Soundings

Issue 4

The Public Good

EDITORS
Stuart Hall
Doreen Massey
Michael Rustin

GUEST EDITOR
Maureen Mackintosh

POETRY EDITOR
Carole Satyamurti

ART EDITORS
Jan Brown and Tim Davison

EDITORIAL OFFICE
Lawrence & Wishart
99a Wallis Road
London E9 5LN

MARKETING CONSULTANT
Mark Perryman

Soundings is published three
times a year, in autumn,
spring and summer by:
Soundings Ltd
c/o Lawrence & Wishart
99a Wallis Road
London E9 5LN

ADVERTISEMENTS
Write for information to Soundings,
c/o Lawrence & Wishart

SUBSCRIPTIONS
1997 subscription rates are (for three issues):
UK: Institutions £70, Individuals £35
Rest of the world: Institutions £80, Individuals £45

BOOKS FOR REVIEW
Contact Soundings Books Editor,
c/o Lawrence & Wishart

ISSN 1362 6620
ISBN 0 85315 836 3

Text setting Art Services, Norwich
Cover photograph: © David Gibson

Printed in Great Britain by
Cambridge University Press, Cambridge

CONTENTS

—————————— *Continued overleaf* ——————————

Continued from previous page

NOTES ON CONTRIBUTORS

Michael Kenny lectures in Politics at the University of Sheffield

Anne Phillips is Professor of Politics at London Guildhall University. Her most recent book is *The Politics of Presence* (OUP 1995).

Paul Hirst is Professor of Social Theory at Birkbeck College, University of London. His books include *Associative Democracy* (Polity 1994) and, with Grahame Thompson, *Globalisation in Question* (Polity 1996).

Grahame Thompson is Senior Lecturer in Social Sciences at the Open University and is editor of *Economy and Society*. He is author, with Paul Hirst, of *Globalisation in Question* (Polity 1996).

Liudmila Vasileva is a Russian artist living in Bulgaria. She recently had an exhibition of her work in Sofia.

Richard Minns is working on regional development in Bulgaria. He is former Joint Chief Executive of Greater London Enterprise Board.

Maura Dooley is author of the collection *Explaining Magnetism* (1991) and *Kissing a Bone* (1996).

Tanya Stepan was born in the United States in 1971. This is her first published poem.

Gregory Warren Wilson is author of the collections *Preserving Lemons* and *Hanging Windchimes in a Vacuum*.

Elizabeth Bartlett has published six collections of poetry, of which the latest is *Two Women Dancing* (Bloodaxe,1995).

Roy Blackman is co-editor of the poetry magazine, *Smith's Knoll*. His first poetry collection is *As Lords Expected* (1996).

Richard Levins is a biologist, active in many fields. He has farmed in Puerto Rico and taught in New York, Cuba and Boston.

Gail Lewis is a Lecturer in Social Policy at the Open University.

Francie Lund is Senior Research Fellow, Centre for Social and Development Studies, University of Natal, South Africa. In the first half of 1996, she chaired the Lund Committee on Child and Family Welfare.

Maureen Mackintosh is Professor of Economics at the Open University.

Pam Smith is Visiting Research Fellow, School of Health, University of Greenwich. She is the author of *The Emotional Labour of Nursing* (Macmillan 1992).

Loretta Loach is a journalist.

John Clarke is author, with Janet Newman, of *The Managerial State* (Sage, forthcoming). He is a Senior Lecturer in Social Policy at the Open University.

Jane Falkingham is a Lecturer in Population Studies at the London School of Economics.

Paul Johnson is a Reader in Economic History at the London School of Economics.

Will Hutton is editor of the *Observer*, and author of *The State We're In* (Vintage 1996).

Charlie King is a researcher at the GMB. He was for eleven years a trustee of the British Gas Pension Fund.

Anne Simpson is Executive Director of PIRC (Pensions and Investment Research Consultants Limited).

Brigid Benson is an Independent Financial Advisor and Principal of GAEIA (Global and Ethical Investment Advice).

Candy Stokes is freelance journalist writing on health and consumer issues.

Anne Showstack Sassoon is Professor of Politics, and Director of the European Research Centre, at Kingston University.

Sarabajaya Kumar is a Research Associate at the Voluntary and Non-profit Research Unit at Aston University, and a Research Fellow at South Bank University.

Ann Hudock is at the Institute of Development Studies at Sussex University; her book on non-governmental organisations (forthcoming, Polity) is entitled *NGOs: Sustainable Idealism?*

Carlo Borzaga teaches economic policy and labour economics at the University of Trento, Italy.

John Stewart is Professor of Local Government and Administration in the Department of Local Government Studies at the University of Birmingham.

The Clintonisation of Labour

The nearer the general election, and the long-awaited moment of a change of government, the more worrying the prospect. This is the sad situation that now faces us in Britain.

This should be a moment of great opportunity, of political transformation. Thatcherism seemed to have almost foundered, kept afloat only by the expedient of throwing its leader overboard. The government has been so far behind in the polls that it will take a record-breaking swing to bring them back to within sight of victory. The Conservative Party is viscerally divided over issues of Europe and national identity which show no sign of going away. Surely, in these circumstances, there has been the space for the Labour Party to construct for itself a programme, to find some coherent ideas to guide it, to offer the electorate some new understanding of the world, and to identify some solid social forces which might sustain its project? In all these respects, something which might actually justify the name New Labour would be welcome.

But instead, New Labour has been constructed largely as a marketing strategy, a piece of political image-making. It insistently defines itself, in a routine that has continued from where Neil Kinnock left off, against what it brands as 'Old Labour'. The dominating principle of this politics is 'realism', as Tony Blair often reminds us. There is said to be no point in a politics of sentiment, in being condemned to further decades of impotent opposition. But the tactical realism of electoral politics, which is understandable enough, masks a realism of a deeper kind - New Labour's belief that little or nothing can be done to alter the substance of post-Thatcher capitalism.

Tony Blair, as Martin Jacques has recently observed (*Guardian*, September 26, 1996), has been triumphantly successful in his project for transforming the Labour Party, but less so in evolving a project for the country. But it is precisely because his project is perceived to remove all serious threat to the dominant order that it has been given such a smooth ride. Its air of inevitability, its success in positioning sceptics as mere fundamentalists and malcontents, derives from its convergence with the main flow of marketisation. New Labour is one successful outcome of Thatcherism - the very political position the right's more far-sighted strategists wanted Labour to take up. The purpose of the new right's project was not, after all, to keep the Conservative Party in office for ever, but to establish a social and economic regime, based on individualism, the market, and a State which would uphold these. What does it matter, from this perspective, that New Labour eventually gets its turn in office, once it has been made to abandon all its earlier commitments to equality, or, in more moderate form, to a changed balance of wealth and power? What it has been induced to jettison is not just 'economic determinism' - who would mind that? - but the basic socialist idea that economic power really matters.

It is because the ruling political discourse has set such iron limits on what New Labour believes it is politically possible to say that Labour has in fact become so reliant on Tony Blair's personality, on belief in his moral integrity (rooted in Christian belief), on ethical declarations which entail no definite commitments, and on a vacuous rhetoric of newness and youth. If Old Labour resorted often enough to one kind of nostalgic sentimentalism, New Labour depends no less on its own inspirational kind.

It becomes clearer as the days pass, that this project is not merely being invented before our eyes, though it has its moments of frenetic improvisation (e.g. the fiasco of the Scottish referendum, in which Labour's capacity to panic from inside an impregnable position will have given the Tories fresh hope even in Scotland). There is a precedent being followed, and as so often in British politics, it comes from the United States. What we are seeing, in sum, is the Clintonisation of British Labour.

What does this process consist of? In the first place, the casting-off of as much of the Labour Party's political and institutional inheritance as can be got rid of -

its constitution, the power of its policy-making conference, the weight of trade union influence in its decision-making, the very idea of a politics of class, and of a principled democratic counter-balance to capitalism. It is reportedly Clinton's strategy to position himself at the apex of a triangle the other points of which are the Democratic and the Republican Parties, cherry-picking the most popular policies from each. This has been the contribution of a new breed of non-partisan political advisers, who switch between parties as opportunity serves them. He is said to have been shaped in his formation by political scientists for whom the normal condition of capitalist democracy is two competing parties, differing not in programme or philosophy, but merely in inflection and style.

It is not difficult to see this as the emergent politics of New Labour, even though the approach here still retains a gloss of innocence - the Bambi factor - which no-one any longer associates with Clinton, if they ever did. New Labour does not contest the moderate right's economic agenda, and some even dream of a realignment that might bring Kenneth Clarke on to our side. The imperatives of keeping taxation down at all costs, of leaving all the privatised utilities in private hands, of giving priority to low levels of inflation and low government deficits - in short 'of maintaining business confidence' - are policies adopted or retained from the right, as a condition of electability and perhaps of governability.

These constraints leave little scope for a coherent programme of reform. Lacking a programme for its full term of office, Labour instead offers a list of 'five early pledges', acknowledging by these few specifics the growing anxiety that it might not do anything significant at all.

'There is no alternative', one almost hears, in a reincarnation of Mrs Thatcher's famous TINA. But this only shows new Labour's failure of imagination. Tony Blair said, in defence of not significantly increasing present levels of taxation, that there was no point in raising taxation to increase the social benefit of the unemployed, since what the unemployed want is to work. But it is obvious that to increase employment requires expenditure too, if on investment rather than on welfare. It would be possible, surely, to say that whilst the total level of taxation, as a proportion of national income, would not increase under Labour its *distribution* certainly will change, in the direction of greater equity. But of this, hardly a word. The risk of offence to the 120,000 citizens who earn more than £100,000 per annum has so far outweighed identification with the millions on average or near-average incomes, not to mention the third of the country living in poverty.

New Labour bases itself on one rising form of institutional power in contemporary capitalism. It is, or intends to be, a post-modern and post-industrial regime, in its recognition of the power of image and information to construct and determine political reality. The role of the 'spin-doctors' and media experts in New Labour is not merely a quirk, an accident of Islington life, or a tactical choice. It represents the rising power of a new social technology, the technology of information and its management.

Previous radical coalitions each relied on a particular institutional and social base to sustain their reforming programmes. These included, at different times: Non-Conformity; a newly mobilised mass democracy; the role of the State and its functionaries as the guarantors of social cohesion and the strength of the nation; the organised working class; and an emergent class of newly-educated professionals in the 1960s and 1970s. Collectivist liberals, the post-war Labour Government, and Wilson's creative blend of what we might now call Old and New Labour, represented these forces in different mixes.

New Labour has no confident relation to any organised constituency. It is positively afraid of the damage that will be done to it electorally if it shows any undue affinity with the state, or with the institutions of the working class. So it constructs its potential following in more individualised ways, addressing both presumed aspirations (the language of opportunities) and anxieties (the language of community, attachment, and social discipline). What is used to bind these atomised constituencies together, given that there are few institutions to do it, is the technology of communication. New Labour seeks to construct, and maintain, a 'virtual' majority.

This form of power unavoidably displaces others. The face-to-face institution of the party branch, or the trade union meeting, a sort of deliberative democracy and delegation, however imperfect, becomes secondary to the individual ballot and the referendum. The subscription previously painstakingly collected by ward treasurer, or automatically checked off as an expression of the power of the union in the workplace, is solicited instead by direct mail. Funding is sought through the clueless patter of telephone fund-raisers. We members will each, individually, be able to vote this year for the Manifesto, for the first time. But this methodology will not allow us to discriminate between policies. Such ballots, since there is only one option to choose from, are little more than a loyalty test. The party leadership go round the country, meeting the membership, in larger and perhaps more interactive meetings than their predecessors did. But these meetings have no power. They can inform the leadership about the state of one particular body of opinion (the party membership), they can suggest some new options for the market researchers to test out. But they leave the leadership to make up its own mind, no longer as the delegated representatives of a constituted assembly. The decision to ignore the vote for the National Executive, and downgrade Clare Short despite her third place in the poll, was a signal of this emerging system. It is a new kind of plebiscitary politics which is being constructed. It is made possible by the new sophistication and efficiency of communications technologies, and their swamping of more conventional and pedestrian channels of influence.

We write on the eve of the Labour Party Conference, which looks as if it may be the final showdown for the politics of Old Labour. Will the trade unions, already being shown the door, administer some last defeat to the New Labour leadership, for example on the level of the minimum wage? Will the ageing heart of Old Labour, in the person of Barbara Castle, win a majority for the principle that pensions should be linked to rising average earnings?

We hope so, but we fear that it may, in the event, make little difference even if this happens. We doubt that the leadership of the Labour Party any longer accepts the idea that its programme should be mandated by its Conference, or that it should be any more accountable to the party membership than to other key interest-groups. Just as Bill Clinton regards the Democratic Party as just one interest, to be balanced as necessary against others, so we think Tony Blair and his advisers regard themselves as accountable not to their party, but to whatever 'virtual' majority they can construct. These rulers call upon the testimony of marketing professionals, as Caesar called upon soothsayers, to legitimise what they do. If they obtain office, they will have acquired sufficient mandate, and other claims to accountability will be defined as secondary. Defeats at Conference on policy issues will be deemed to be non-binding, and will be finessed, or forgotten.

These, if we are right about them, are major changes in our political system. These political technologies are designed to include some voices and interests, and to exclude others. There is an inescapable conjunction between the trimming of Labour's programme towards the norms of the market, and these changes in the institutional forms of the party and its mode of domination. New Labour's courting of the corporations, not only on issues of policy, but also in the soliciting of funds, is another aspect of Clintonisation. Labour wishes to position itself as but one of two parties which can equally claim and receive the support of business. This is a significant retreat not only from the goal of long-term socialist transformation, but even from the will to constitute a democratic balance or counter-weight to the power of capital.

We shall return to these themes in later issues, including the question of what Labour's 'project for the country' ought to be. Meanwhile we point to the necessity to maintain and develop such democratic spaces as one can, including those within the Labour Party itself.

After the deluge
Politics and civil society in the wake of the New Right

Michael Kenny

Michael Kenny *argues that the different parties in recent debates over community share the assumption that we are now witnessing the triumph of civil society over the state. Tracing the origins and evolution of these claims, he discusses the problems of looking at social change in this way, and critically analyses some contemporary conceptions of civil society.*

The rise of civil society?

One of the most important themes in contemporary politics concerns the apparent failure of the New Right to capture the hearts and minds of significant sections of the British population and to reshape society in its own image. Does this signify the residually left-wing commitments of the nation, manifested for instance in continuing support for the welfare state? Or might this suggest the emergence of a new era in British political history, characterised by the consolidation of a dense and vibrant civil society which is now so complex and autonomous that any state-led attempt to reshape the patterns and relations of life within this realm is now impossible? The latter argument carries great force in present circumstances. It connects with the prevailing mood of disillusion with the conventional political system and the declining faith in public institutions and representatives noted by commentators across the political spectrum. This type of argument appears to reinforce both the communitarianism advocated by New Labour and the libertarian anti-statism which radical intellectuals on the left have advocated since the 1960s.

If this does represent a plausible reading of recent political developments, some uncomfortable questions arise. If political life in the 1990s involves the triumph of civil society over the state, what implications does this have for conventional definitions of what both the left and right in British politics stand for? If it is accurate to argue that civil society is now the primary sphere within modern political life, what does this mean for those forces of the left which have historically viewed their role in terms of the capture of state power through electoral means, and the deployment of its instruments to socially progressive and economically just ends? Both of these questions have informed Tony Blair's current efforts to renovate and modernise the culture and organisation of the Labour Party.

Labour in British society

Blair's ideas emerge in part from a tradition with its roots outside the Labour Party. The idea that new sorts of issues and campaigns are displacing the old political forms has been an important catalyst for the re-emergence of the notion of civil society on the left since the 1960s. Until recently, arguments about the increasing importance of movements emerging outside the political system, as well as debates concerning the value of communities in social life, took place in intellectual circles outside the party. Whilst Labour has been deeply shaped by the particular evolution of Britain's social and economic history and political culture, it has historically drawn strength from cutting the party off from trends, movements and cultures beyond itself. To some extent this was a necessary part of the process of seeking and maintaining an independent identity. In other respects it marked a deep suspicion towards other political struggles and forces, especially those which have remained beyond its immediate sphere of influence.

Despite the heterogeneity of social interests which the party has incorporated throughout the century, it has adopted structures and developed a culture which sustain a highly statist conception of political change and social action. These features have frustrated radicals since the party's inception. One of the most radical aspects of Tony Blair's reforming project stems from his attack upon Labour members' instinctive reliance upon the state to provide solutions to contemporary social problems, as well as his desire to reshape the insular culture which prevails in Labour's ranks. This project, sometimes caricatured as a knee-jerk imitation of New Right ideological commitments, actually carries echoes of longstanding radical criticisms of the party's culture and structures, though earlier radicals never imagined that such changes would be so energetically pursued by the party's elite. One of the most longstanding and debilitating consequences of the capture of the Labour Party by the culture of labourism has been the distance between its policy thinking and deep-seated changes within Britain's society and economy in the last thirty years.

This gap has encouraged a series of radical ventures which have emerged from within the party and beyond. These have sought to reform or reconstitute party culture and organisation - from the New Left of the early 1960s to Charter '88, the magazine *Marxism Today* and the SDP of the 1980s. Each in their very different ways tried to reconnect the party to the energies and aspirations of groups beyond its boundaries. All were fascinated by social change, sharing the conviction that Labour had lost touch with the real story of British fortunes in the post-war period - including the relative decline of its industrial performance, and the impact of important social changes which were producing identities and concerns within the social arena from which the party remained aloof. Each of these currents has in different ways provided ingredients for the Blairite programme. One important point of intersection between these different reforming ventures has been their advocacy of the concept of civil society, to signify both the realms of life which the left should be addressing, and the kind of broad political coalition which it needed to envisage.

The new left alternative

The first generation of the New Left in the late 1950s began the process of thinking through the limitations of Labour's statism. In doing so the movement's leading intellectuals anticipated many subsequent arguments on the left about civil society. A particularly important aspect of its politics stemmed from the internationally comparative approach it adopted in its analysis of British society. Youthful New Left devotees in the early 1960s were more excited by the civil rights struggles in the southern states of the United States, revolts against French colonial rule in Algeria, the popular uprisings launched against Soviet rule in Hungary, and the disastrous Suez expedition, than by events at home, though the emergence of the first wave of CND provided some kind of indigenous equivalent. This international outlook was an important feature of the 'new politics' which the New Left pioneered, and shaped the notions of protest, political action and social space which became issues of great interest to subsequent generations. For the first time in the post-war period, Britain's patterns of social and economic development were systematically and unfavourably compared with events elsewhere. And an important lineage of thinking was established, about the relationships between the 'ancien regime' entrenched in the British state and faltering economic performance (ironically in a period when the British economy was positively robust in comparison with subsequent developments).[1] This has become a rich and highly influential source of debate and reflection, providing one of the points of origin of Will Hutton's recent best-seller, *The State We're In*.[2] Debates sponsored by the early New Left have become the staples of today: is British culture being remorselessly Americanised? is consumerism eroding older social values? can the ethos of community offer forms of resistance to the new economic forces and values sweeping across British society? The origins of the contemporary civil society tradition are worth noting because of the extent to which aspects of this agenda have been lost in latter-day discussions.

> 'Debates sponsored by the early New Left have become the staples of today'

The new social movements

The New Left were by no means the only grouping on the political scene of the 1960s to assert their distaste for the limitations of the political system. The 'new' movements which arose in different ways from the radical milieu of student politics in the 1960s, notably the women's and anti-Vietnam war movements, began to reshape the landscape of modern British politics. So too did the anti-racist, lesbian and gay, and different environmentalist campaigns of subsequent decades, though the second wave of CND in the early 1980s was perhaps the most spectacularly influential of all these movements. These and other new campaigns and struggles have all developed in divergent directions, and have their own complicated histories. Yet all share a similar rejection of the narrowness

1. Perry Anderson, 'Origins of the Present Crisis', *New Left Review* 23, 1964; Tom Nairn, *The Breakup of Britain*, New Left Books, London 1977.
2   Will Hutton, *The State We're In*, Jonathan Cape, London 1995.

of the terms of debate in the political mainstream. One of the most important aspects of these movements was the sense of worth they attached to domains previously downgraded in political analysis - the everyday, the emotional, and the non-human environment for example. The particular challenges that they have in different ways posed to British institutions and culture make them more than single-issue adjuncts to the political systems - a rather patronising description with which are they often labelled. For example, under the influence of movements such as feminism and anti-racism, it has been far less plausible to regard society as a passive, malleable sphere, organised around pre-given identities that the party in power can manipulate at will.

The Gramscian tradition

The New Left's emphases on both understanding and mobilising within civil society carried far more conviction in the wake of these movements which refused to play by conventional political rules and explicitly sought to reshape values and cultures. The notion of civil society thus came into vogue in the 1970s, following the dissemination of the ideas of the Italian Marxist theorist Antonio Gramsci. Gramsci conceived civil society as the defining characteristic of states in Western Europe, famously conceptualising the different institutions, cultures and practices which constituted this realm in the language of military strategy. His ideas about the war of position which the left needed to conduct across a range of fronts contributed to some important rethinking of socialist goals and political tactics. This perspective reached its apogee in the 1980s as Thatcherism sought to build exactly the kind of hegemonic project throughout civil society that those influenced by Gramsci had begun to envisage. Seeking to reshape the prevailing patterns of values and identities within the nation in conjunction with its radical governmental programme, the New Right sought to embed its core values in the 'common sense' of everyday life, articulated in an expressive and popular vernacular. It also tried to reposition the different social identities prevalent within British society around its own rather crude politics of identity - stressing a highly exclusive conception of the English nation, a narrow conception of 'economic man', and calling for the renovation of some deeply conservative moral traditions. Labour's apparent inability to understand, let alone respond to, these disturbing moves, returned civil society decisively to the political agenda of many radicals. These themes were explored throughout this period in the journal *Marxism Today*.

The 'left conservative' position

The experiences of Thatcherism have also encouraged a rather different interpretation of concepts such as civil society and community.

The response of some intellectuals to the changes wrought by Thatcherism has been to suggest that Labour should now occupy the conservative flank in British politics. Whilst the radical right sought to open both economy and society to the cold winds of global competition and seemed to care little about the deep divisions and different forms of social exclusion which these processes have brought, the left has been increasingly tempted to stand for what is permanent and continuous in people's lives, offering security and tradition in the wake of the 'permanent revolution' which the New Right oversaw.[3] Community, in Blair's hands, offers a similar emphasis upon a comforting past characterised by stability and order. These ideas draw on a quite different lineage of civil society theory, which has been championed by more explicitly conservative advocates of the merits and stability provided by specifically English social institutions and values.

These different views by no means exhaust the different usages of civil society discourse. But both represent highly influential interpretations of it, and illustrate the potency of the view that politics needs to be fundamentally reconceived in the wake of the triumph of civil society. Some proponents of these ideas regarded the seismic political events of 1989 as signalling not just the demise of state-sponsored socialism but the final victory of civil society over modern states; some deemed it 'natural' that citizens should desire to live in a rich, multifarious and pluralistic social environment in which their varied needs and identities are addressed within different institutional contexts. According to this line of argument, all totalising ideologies which seek to establish fixed identities for individuals and rigid forms of social closure have become redundant. The notion of a political project from above which harnesses and reorganises the identities of its subjects to its own ends is thus increasingly problematic. Simultaneously, the legitimacy of the state, in a whole range of functions such as policing, welfare provision, and education, has become much harder to secure. For many, these changes now provide the defining political theme of the age - the limitations of state dirigisme in social and economic policy combined with a rejection of grand ideological visions

---

3. Anthony Giddens, 'What's left for Labour?', *New Statesman and Society*, 30 September 1994.

and programmes. These and other related arguments point to the resurgence of civil society as one of the central phenomena of late modern politics.

This has been reflected since the mid-1980s in the growth of intellectual interest in this topic, reaching a crescendo with the publication of texts like John Keane's impressive edited collection, *Civil Society and the State*.[4] Increasing attention has been paid to the limitations of state activity in societies on both the left and right, as well as the extent to which the preservation,

'The notion of a political project from above is increasingly problematic'

enlargement and diversification of civil society represents important ways forward for democratic politics. The development of civil societies 'like ours' featured prominently in academic and political discussions of the processes of democratisation in contexts such as Latin America in the 1980s and Eastern Europe after 1989.

The trouble with civil society

Though there are too many variants of these arguments to elaborate here, some shared, and highly problematic, assumptions underpin the resurgence of civil society and communitarian discourse. A common belief is that these represent relatively benign, and sometimes inherently progressive spaces. In the 'left conservative' version of this argument, the institutions which embody security and maintain continuity in social life have tended to be assumed rather than analysed. But for the new movements which have appeared since the 1960s, it is exactly these institutions and their cultures which need to be challenged - from the House of Lords to the model of the nuclear family. As feminism in particular has shown, the ways in which power is dispersed throughout social domains engenders a continual process of negotiation, containment and occasionally explicit conflict.

For those who have stressed the organic connections between the growth of the new social movements and the emergence of powerful civil societies, some equally unhelpful assumptions prevail, not least the view that the concerns of these movements might contribute to a coherent alternative politics which takes place outside the state. A careful examination of the different circumstances in which new movements have emerged reveals the degree to which their fortunes have

4.   John Kean (ed), *Civil Society and the State: New European Perspectives*, Verso, London 1988.

of consumerism as an important social practice illustrates the weaknesses of conceiving only non-economic spheres as ones where moral values apply. The growth of 'ethical consumerism' is one of the most important phenomena of our times.

Rethinking citizenship

The notions of civil society and community have opened all sorts of conceptual and political doors for the left. Both have offered the theoretical possibility of resolving the increasingly marked tensions between individual interests and the public good which characterise contemporary social development. As different commentators have observed, a commitment to a truly civic society implies the creation of collective values and an ethos of public service and participation which works against the acquisitive and self-interested privatism at the heart of late modern societies. Whilst sections of the left began to grapple with these difficult issues towards the end of the 1980s, a model of citizenship appropriate to the patterns of social life which will prevail in the twenty-first century remains elusive. Blair's communitarianism is one response to this problem, representing a bold reassertion of the bonds and loyalties that bind individuals in their very most immediate locales. But whether this offers more than a nostalgic fantasy in the context of the irreversible changes which have occurred in the last twenty years remains less clear.

For thinkers like Gramsci, or the contemporary Italian theorist Norberto Bobbio, the notion of civil society has allowed a deeper analytical engagement with the complex ways in which social identities are produced in modern societies. But this emphasis appears to have been lost in some recent invocations of the term. In particular, the complex interactions between the different domains of power which shape individual identities, as well as the changing relationships between institutions and individuals, are the axes along which some of the most important changes in recent times have occurred. Debates about citizenship or community need to incorporate the very different contexts in which individuals operate, as well as the various locations at which identities are formed and contested - simultaneously through urban subcultures, national cultural affiliations, and global concerns, for example. The problem for advocates of civil society is that this concept and its related values were first developed by thinkers of earlier eras who were far more confident about the common interests and values which could underpin a model of citizenship which was meaningful to all. These assumptions have been substantially undermined by the complex patterns of differentiation prevalent in late twentieth-century social life. The different forms and levels of contemporary social interaction have to be brought into any meaningful model of the public good in the civil society of the next century.

Bringing the state back in

In general, the dualistic conception of states and societies which the notion of civil society has sometimes encouraged offers a rather inadequate framework for understanding political and social life. Given the changes in state-society relationships typical of all industrialised states in the 1980s, this is especially so. The state's involvement in its subjects' lives is today far more extensive and pervasive than at any previous period, despite the widespread acceptance of the state's limitations in so many fields. Whilst civil society has undoubtedly grown more diverse, rich and dense in its institutional networks and sub-cultural possibilities, and includes cultures which have become tremendously fragmented, the state's dealings with society have become more extensive and restrictive in areas of personal morality and behaviour. Yet, simultaneously, the legitimacy of state intervention in some spheres of social and economic life has been substantially eroded. This last development is perhaps the most powerful factor undermining a conception of politics based on a counterposition between civil society, or community, and the state. The linkages between these spheres cannot be registered by arguments which assume a neat division between them. The analysis of radicals now has to reflect the contours of the new political economy which will characterise the twenty-first century: the artificial separation of state, economy and society not only hinders a proper understanding of the world into which we are moving, but hampers our conception of the kind of politics which can genuinely provide alternatives at different locations and scales of social life.

In particular, the premature death notices which have appeared for the nation state represent a misleading gloss on some complex developments. In Britain especially, as David Marquand and Anthony Wright have argued, a tremendous degree of power remains within the confines of the state.[7] Even in terms of the agendas developed by the most radical movements in civil society, the state implicitly figures as a social and economic regulator, as the potential guarantor of hard-won equality legislation, or, in the case of the environment, as a key agent in

---

7. David Marquand and Anthony Wright, 'Commentary: After Clause Four', *Political Quarterly*, 66, 3, 1995, pp121-5.

denied by some. But the ambivalence which characterises the response of many 'radicals' to Blair, is an indication of the recognition of aspects of this radical lineage in his politics, combined with a lingering suspicion about his political goals and motives.

But in other respects, New Labour's instincts remain deeply attuned to the rhythms and assumptions of a highly centralised and increasingly insular political system. New Labour has not broken from old Labour when it comes to thinking about political change. Blair and those around him might usefully heed a wider set of heterodox political voices from outside the party's inner circle. One intellectual current to which they might turn consists of New Left thinkers who have rejected labourist thinking throughout the last thirty years, and have explored the problems of state legitimacy, the need for a hegemonic conception of politics to provide a coherent philosophical underpinning for any new policy programme, and the centrality of the state within the unusual pattern of British economic and political development. Blair's communitarianism might therefore be supplemented with the recognition that bridges of trust, accountability and consent need to be rebuilt between public institutions and social groups - inherently difficult and painful tasks in this context. Equally, the significant potential for state-led modernisation in Britain was powerfully illustrated by the Thatcher governments. Both the globalisation thesis and the communitarian argument can provide easy ways of avoiding facing up to the realities, possibilities and dangers of state power.

Both the New Left and civil society lineages have rightly pointed to the increasing diversity of both the social terrain and the politics of opposition within modern societies. This emphasis might be usefully taken on board to supplant the traditional way in which the new forces emerging in British society are treated: campaigns, protest groups and voluntary associations whose political allegiances are not immediately obvious are generally regarded as single-issue supplicants within the Blair camp. Contact with these forces, according to this mentality, means electoral risk and future claims on the public purse. Blair may be right that economic realities dictate that expectations of what a Labour government can deliver need to be held within realistic boundaries. But securing and maintaining a popular mandate for a new policy agenda requires a more extensive dialogue with a diverse coalition of social groups and their representatives.

Thanks to Andrew Gamble, Mike Harris, Nick Stevenson and the Soundings *editors for their comments on an earlier draft of this article.*

What has socialism to do with sexual equality?

Anne Phillips

Anne Phillips looks at current debates on equality and gender in the socialist tradition.

The place of equality in socialist thinking is itself a pretty tangled issue. In fact, this article began life as part of a discussion to establish what, if anything, remained the distinctively *socialist* contribution to our understanding of equality.[1] Bearing this in mind, we may also ask what has socialism to do with *sexual* equality? At the most general level, we could say that equality is central to socialism, and that equality includes equality between women and men. But the meaning of equality has been widely contested, and this level of generality does not take us very far. Karl Marx was always rather sniffy about empty claims to equality, and his preferred objective - 'from each according to his ability, to each according to his needs' - seems entirely compatible with a division of labour that allocates different responsibilities to women and men. Later socialists have been more willing make equality a core value, but they have disagreed over the appropriate balance between

---

1. This discussion was organised by IPPR, in a series of seminars entitled 'Back to Basics', largely in response to the Commission on Social Justice, whose report drew heavily, for its philosophical underpinnings, on recent developments in liberal theory. The papers from this series will be published by the IPPR in a book entitled *Equality* in 1997.

equality of opportunity and equality of outcomes, and they have varied widely in their understanding of what it is that has to be equalised. The idea that domestic work, for example, should be distributed equally between women and men, was a relatively late development even in feminist circles: as Ellen DuBois has noted in her discussion of nineteenth century suffragists, '"sharing housework" may be a more uniquely twentieth-century feminist demand than "smashing monogamy"'.[2]

Sexual equality in the socialist and liberal traditions

Equalising either housework or childcare certainly did not figure large in nineteenth century socialist debate. The so-called utopian socialists tended to favour co-operative arrangements for domestic work or bringing up children. But this derived from their critique of the privatised (self-interested) family, rather than any preoccupation with redistributing work between women and men.[3] Later in the century, Marxists tended to regard women's confinement to the domestic sphere as the key factor in their subordination to men, and looked to the fuller participation of women in socialised production as the means to their emancipation. In Engels' over-optimistic extrapolation from the employment of women in the textile industry, this process was already well underway; in August Bebel's *Women and Socialism*, the emancipation through work had to be combined with a programme for socialising domestic labour.[4] Instead of each woman being condemned to her own private oven and sink, there would be central kitchens and public laundries. That the cooks and the cleaners might continue to be women was not, at this stage, considered an issue.

The alternative argument from the nineteeenth century was that a genuinely unconfined free market should be enough to deliver sexual equality. This, largely, is what John Stuart Mill argued in his essay on *The Subjection of Women* (published in 1869), where he identified the subjection of women as the main surviving remnant of an earlier social order, and increasingly at odds with the defining principle of modern society. He took this to be the notion that competition and not birth should be what dictates a person's position in life: that instead of our

2. Ellen DuBois, 'The Radicalism of the Woman Suffrage Movement: Notes Toward the Reconstruction of Nineteenth-Century Feminism', *Feminist Studies* 3, 1/2 (1975) p66.
3. For the Owenite approach to these issues, see Barbara Taylor, *Eve and the New Jerusalem*, Virago 1983.
4. First published in 1883, subsequently revised in 1891 and 1895.

life-chances being determined by the accidents of birth, what we do or become should be a matter that is decided by free competition. 'Nobody,' as Mill put it, 'thinks it necessary to make a law that only a strong-armed man shall be a blacksmith. Freedom and competition suffice to make blacksmiths strong armed men, because the weak-armed can earn more by engaging in occupations for which they are more fit.'[5] What, then, was added by the plethora of nineteenth century legislation that prohibited women from even entering the competitive arena? If the principle of freedom and competition is true, he argued, 'we ought to act as if we believed it, and not to ordain that to be born a girl instead of a boy, any more than to be born black instead of white, or a commoner instead of a nobleman, shall decide the person's position through all life - shall interdict people from all the more elevated social positions, and from all, except a few, respectable occupations (p448).

As is apparent from some of his other writings, Mill was not an unambiguous supporter of free competition. He was also very much taken with the case for co-operative ownership, and he sympathised with many of the socialist arguments of his contemporaries. As far as sexual equality was concerned, however, he did seem to think an unconfined free market - unconfined, that is, by legislation that dictated differential treatment for women and men - should be enough to deliver the desired result. Mill neither anticipated nor desired a world in which men and women would take on the same range of work or responsibilities; he did not expect men to take an equal share of domestic work or childcare; and in common with many economists of his time (and later), he believed that too great an influx of women into the labour market would drag down wage levels and make everyone substantially worse off. What mattered was that women should be educated and enabled to support themselves, freed from the legal prohibitions that limited their educational and job opportunities, and released from the inequities in marriage law that made marriage a relationship between master and slave. But once marriage and motherhood had been transformed into a genuinely free choice and consensual arrangement, he expected the majority of women to opt gladly for their conventional role.

If we take these as exemplars of the more sexually egalitarian wings of the socialist and liberal traditions, it is evident that both traditions can generate a

---

7.   J.S.Mill, 'The Subjection of Women', in Mill, *Three Essays*, OUP, 1975, p447.

commitment to sexual equality. Whatever the historical errors or theoretical failings in Engels' *Origin of the Family, Private Property and the State* (published in 1884), no one reading his analysis of male domination and female subjugation can doubt the importance he attached to achieving equality between women and men. And while the popularity of *Women and Socialism* owed more to its much-needed vision of the future socialist society than to its specific arguments on women, the book

'**Both the socialist and liberal traditions can generate a commitment to sexual equality**'

went through more than fifty editions before Bebel's death in 1913 to become one of the most widely read texts in the German socialist movement. John Stuart Mill's writings on sexual equality attracted less contemporary attention that his other works on political theory or political economy, but his consistent backing for most of the central campaigns

of nineteenth century feminism helped secure a close relationship between liberalism and first wave feminism. Neither the socialist nor the liberal tradition has proved itself a strong or consistent supporter of sexual equality; but both can make some claim to being its 'natural home'.

If there is any basis, from this earlier period, for claiming a special affinity with socialism, it lies in the socialist critique of privacy, and the way this alerted socialists to the peculiar constraints of the domestic sphere. Liberals were far more likely to defend private spaces against public regulation, and much less likely to regard the household as a place of confinement. Even allowing for John Stuart Mill's strong condemnation of marital slavery, this made them more inclined to accept some version of 'separate spheres'. Socialists, by contrast, tended to distrust privacy as inherently individualistic and limiting, and in their celebration of collective activity and socialised production, they were considerably more disparaging of domestic life. For many, this simply spilled over into a disdain for women. For the minority, however, who bothered to address the so-called 'Woman Question', it generated more consistent support for women's entry into the labour market than yet figured in the liberal tradition, as well as more imaginative proposals for transforming the conditions under which domestic work was carried out. The difference between the two traditions has sometimes been theorised as a difference between pursuing equality of opportunities and achieving equality of outcomes: liberalism typically focussing on removing the *legal* constraints to free up equality of opportunities; socialism typically addressing the *structural* conditions that are necessary to substantial equality. But in its origins, at least, the difference stems as much from the liberal defence of private spaces and the socialist critique of private confinement.

Though the latter offered a basis for allying feminism to the socialist tradition, most of those active in the earlier feminist campaigns found a more congenial home within the liberal camp. Legal constraints and prohibitions were a particularly pressing concern through the late nineteenth century and early twentieth centuries; and while few liberals showed any great enthusiasm for women's emancipation, those who did gave active support to feminist campaigns. Socialists, meanwhile, tended to play the class card to trump any excessive preoccupation with sexual equality. When Selina Cooper, for example, argued the case for women's suffrage at the 1905 Labour Party Conference, Harry Quelch of the (Marxist) Social Democratic Federation announced that 'Mrs Cooper has placed sex first...we have to put Labour first in every case.'[6] In the hierarchy of socialist concerns, sexual equality usually came low down the list.

Affinities with liberalism and socialism in 'second-wave' feminism

A rather different pattern emerged in the early years of the contemporary women's movement, when feminists found themselves more closely attuned to the socialist than the liberal tradition. Debates through the 1970s were often ordered through a three-way split between liberal, socialist and radical feminists; in Britain, far more than in the USA, the overwhelming majority placed themselves in the second or third camp. Previous campaigns had removed many of the more overt legal inequalities, thereby reducing some of the attractions of liberal feminism. But the connections that were made with socialism were also specific to the historical moment, for they reflected a wider political context in which socialism had come to set the terms for radical social critique. Many of the early activists came from a prior involvement in left politics, and even in distancing themselves from socialism, feminists often reproduced its analytical traditions. One of the key texts in the development of a radical (i.e. *non*-socialist) feminism was Shulamith Firestone's *Dialectic of Sex*, but Firestone employed a Marxist terminology to identify women as a

6.   Cited in Jill Liddington, *The Life and Times of a Respectable Rebel: Selina Cooper 1864-1946*,Virago 1984, p165.

distinct 'sex-class'.[7] Several years later, radical feminists in Britain described themselves, somewhat confusingly, as 'revolutionary feminists'. In the formative years of the women's liberation movement, the socialist tradition still had a monopoly on the language of radicalism. The later discovery that the right could also be radical came as rather a shock.

Where there was a more substantial theoretical basis to the partnership of socialism with feminism, it lay in the socialist equation of domesticity with confinement, and the socialist preference for whatever was collective, public, and social. Few feminists went along with the idea that women's emancipation would occur simply through their entry into socialised production. But the notion that sexual inequality was rooted in women's confinement to the private household fitted well with the preoccupations of the 1950s and 60s: the critique of housework, for example, as a thankless and repetitive cycle in which nothing new was ever created; or the critique of the nuclear family, as requiring women to sacrifice their integrity and personality to the nurture of husbands who would come to despise them, and children whose first task on reaching maturity would be to push their mothers aside. Feminists in the 1990s are far more likely to dwell on the double burden women experience in juggling the demands of paid employment with the care responsibilities that continue to fall almost exclusively on their shoulders. In the formative literature, by contrast, attention was focussed on the way that women were silenced, marginalised, turned in on themselves, encouraged to look to fulfilment through finding the 'right man', discouraged from any more public activity. In principle, at least, the liberal language of individuality and freedom offered an equally powerful resource for addressing these issues. But liberalism was regarded as condoning a sharp separation between public and private spheres, and turning a blind eye to what went on in the household. This hardly tuned in with the aspirations of those who were experimenting with alternative forms of collective living and collective childcare, nor did it have much to say to those who were developing an analysis of male violence. (Not that this last was a strong point among socialists either.)

The distance travelled since then is enormous. For feminists, the most important milestones have been the failure to establish sustainable alternatives to the nuclear family; the steady increase in women's paid employment, which has made the double

---

7. Shulamith Firestone, *The Dialectic of Sex*, Jonathan Cape, 1971.

burden so much more central to feminist analysis; and the disenchantment with that combination of full time employment for women, under-staffed and over-regulated nurseries for children, which characterised so many of the state socialist societies. In her periodisation of feminist approaches to motherhood (based on American experience, but comparable to what happened in Britain) Ann Snitow notes the self-questioning of motherhood that characterised so many of the key texts of the 1970s: the attempt to detach being a woman from the requirement to be a mother; but also the attempt to detach biological motherhood from the responsibilities of caring for children.[8] This contrasts markedly with a subsequent celebration of motherhood as generating distinct values of nurturance and care.

In this later phase, the quintessentially feminist programme has been a reorganisation of paid employment (more substantial parental leave, more part-time work for both women and men, more flexibility in employment patterns) so that both mothers *and* fathers can divide their time equitably between parenthood and work. The idea that parenting could be socialised, either through better social provision of child care services, or through collective living arrangements that draw both parents and non-parents into responsibilities for caring for children, has given way to a more privatised scenario, in which individual mothers and fathers will be enabled to reach a more egalitarian division of their domestic labour. Not that social provision has dropped out of the programme: improving and expanding nursery provision, for example, remains a central feminist concern. But feminists are less inclined to view care work just as a 'burden' to be lifted from their shoulders onto those of the state. They are also less prepared to view sexual equality as something that changes women's lives without more substantially changing the men's.

Over the same period, socialists have also made their peace with privacy. It is no longer presumed that social ownership must be better than private; it is no longer presumed that collective arrangements must be better than individual ones; it is no longer presumed that people find their fulfilment in socialised production, or are lessened by watching a video in the privacy of their home. Though the current flurry around community or communitarianism testifies to continuing anxieties about the scale of this shift, most socialists have backed away from the

---

8. Ann Snitow, 'Feminism and Motherhood: An American Reading', *Feminist Review*, Number 40, 1992.

critique of privacy that was so characteristic of the earlier tradition. Most, indeed, have refashioned their socialism to give more place to the individual, and the rights and freedoms of this individual (which may include the right to opt out of trade unions or out of socialised provision in education or health) are now regarded as eminently suitable socialist concerns.

Where does this leave any special affinity between socialism and sexual equality? Oddly, it seems, much stronger. Today's socialists are more consistently attuned to the requirements of sexual equality than their predecessors; and in Britain, as elsewhere in Europe, it has been parties on the left of the political spectrum that have been most willing to adopt measures of positive action to speed up the process of change.[9] The Labour Party is certainly more tuned in than it has been to the issues and problems that confront women, as evidenced in its commitment to recruiting more women as political representatives, and in the impressively 'feminised' understanding of the contemporary labour market that underpins the Report of the Commission on Social Justice. But this growing affinity with sexual equality may owe more to the recent convergence between liberal and socialist values (and the associated downgrading of class) than to anything specific to the socialist tradition. What does socialism have to add to the project of sexual equality? Can sexual equality be achieved within a broadly liberal framework that recognises the equal worth of all individuals, regardless of their sex? Or is socialism - and if so, what kind of socialism - a necessary condition for sexual equality?

Equality in contemporary socialist thinking

In his contribution to the seminar on 'Back to Basics', David Miller argues that the attachment to (some kind of) equality does not uniquely distinguish socialists from their opponents. We might equally well note that the attachment to (some kind of) liberty does not uniquely distinguish liberals from anyone else. Today's socialists are very much preoccupied with the relationship between equality and freedom, and most would like to arrive at some trade-off between these two that weights them relatively evenly. One expression of this is the rather disparaging dismissal of strict equality (the 'leveller's strategy') that we find in the Report of the Commission on Social Justice; another is the recovery of equality of

---

9. See Pippa Norris 'Comparing Legislative Recruitment', in J. Lovenduski and P. Norris (eds), *Gender and Party Politics*, Sage, 1993.

opportunities as a far more radical strategy than its critics used to admit.

Thus the Commission on Social Justice argues for what Stuart White describes as an 'endowment egalitarianism' that equalises the initial distribution of capabilities and skills, primarily through education and training.[10] It presents this as an attractive alternative to the more conventional redistribution of income. If the alternative worked, it would short-circuit the equalisation-after-the-event that characterises policies of progressive taxation. Instead of waiting for the inequalities to emerge - and then taxing the rich to pay for the poor - it should be possible to intervene at an earlier stage to equalise life-chances and job opportunities. What makes this particularly attractive in the present political climate is that it promises to ease the tension between equality and freedom. Instead of relying on an interventionist state to deliver more substantial equality of income, people will be equalised to make their own choices, and make what they can of their lives.

'The Report of the Commission on Social Justice dismisses strict equality rather disparagingly'

Such a strategy is in many ways limited: it seems to accept the slots that are becoming available in an economy that divides jobs more starkly than before into full-time or part-time, high-paid or low-paid, relatively secure or inherently transient, but calls for a more radical understanding of social and job mobility that will empower individuals to move more freely and equally between these slots. That said, the equal opportunities that are implied in the strategy are considerably more substantial that the equal right to enter the competitive arena. They carry with them a strong commitment to eliminating the early patterns of disadvantage that weave their way around children as they enter the educational system, and they anticipate extensive social intervention to equalise initial endowments. The Commission on Social Justice goes, indeed, considerably further even than this, for it construes equal opportunities as including a life-time chance to regain ground that was lost at an earlier stage. The idea is not just to equalise our starting positions, and then condone whatever inequalities subsequently emerge. The emphasis on 'lifelong learning' suggests that some of the subsequent inequalities must also be tackled - particularly those that relate to inequalities in education and skills.

---

10. Stuart White, 'Rethinking the Strategy of Equality: A Critical Appraisal of the Report of the Borrie Commission on Social Justice'. To be published in *Equality*, IPPR, 1997.

All inequalities of power or income must arise either from an inequality in social conditions, or else from an unequal inheritance of capacities and talents, among which we must surely include the capacity for hard work. From a socialist perspective, the first looks self-evidently unjust. The second also seems unfair, for these things are hardly under our control. The problem with the second, however, is that we cannot just legislate all these differences away, for if we did, we would end up eliminating much of what we value in life.

It is not really fair, for example, that those with a gift for language should be better placed to influence decisions than those who find it hard to articulate their opinions, and it is particularly unfair when the class bias in educational opportunities skews this in favour of certain social groups. But even if we managed to eliminate the class bias, there would still be differences of personality and ability that made some individuals more persuasive than others. The only way to eliminate this would be to end all political discussion, and we would hardly be happy with this.[11] It may also seem unfair, to follow a line of argument much loved by Robert Nozick, that an individual born with a Grecian profile should have a better sex life than an individual born with a snub nose.[12] But if the only way to deal with this is to allocate sexual partners at random, thereby eliminating any element of personal choice, we would hardly be happy with this. We cannot legislate against all accidents of birth, and to this extent, we are stuck with some inevitable level of inequality. What we need is some way of distinguishing the inevitable *individual* variations (some people are just more lucky than others) from those associated with more blanket injunctions. From a socialist perspective, this second category would certainly include the disabilities that flow from one's class; it should also include the disabilities that flow from one's sex or the colour of one's skin.

I do not pretend that this is an easy distinction, for all differences between individuals lend themselves to a group classification (the class of people who are tone-deaf, for example, and by virtue of this group characteristic, are denied the chance to work in the music business), and what one person defines as bad luck will be perceived by another as a blanket injunction. I also recognise that arguments for strict equality can be modified by pragmatic concerns. I would argue, for example, that inherited inequalities of wealth are always unjustified, but given the

---

11. This is one of the points made in Ronald Dworkin's 'What is Equality? Part 4: Political Equality', *University of San Francisco Law Review*, Number 22, 1988.
12. Robert Nozick, *Anarchy, State and Utopia*, Basic Books, 1974, esp ch8.

widespread desire to pass on to one's children the benefits built up through one's life, it may be impossible to get majority support for 100% tax on inheritance. In similar vein, I would argue that sexual inequalities in power or income are always unjustified, but I would willingly accept a strategy that started with some initial redistribution and worked up towards equal shares; or that started with increasing the proportion of women in male-dominated occupations, and built up towards full gender parity. In this, as in any area of social policy, one cannot hope to do everything overnight. The final aim, however, must surely be to eliminate inequalities associated with sex. I can see no normative basis for stopping short of full sexual equality.

> 'We cannot legislate all differences away, for if we did, we would end up eliminating much of what we value in life'

Is socialism a condition for sexual equality?

It is at this point that the special affinity between socialism and sexual equality comes more sharply to the fore. Sexual equality, as I understand it, depends on a major restructuring of the relationship between paid and unpaid labour so as to detach this division from the distinction between women and men. Sexual equality cannot be achieved simply through socialised provision of services (more nurseries, more home helps and meals on wheels, more homes for the disabled or the mentally ill or the elderly), for while these can certainly help equalise conditions for women and men, they do so by shifting care responsibilities from women working in the privacy of their home to (usually) women employed by the state. There are necessary limits to this strategy, for none of us wants a world in which care work is entirely institutionalised. The strategy also leaves untouched the differential roles of women and men. It will still be women who do the work; it will still be women who depend on the services. When these are threatened or removed, it will still be women who have to carry the consequences. The longer term solution lies combining socialised care provision with a new balance between paid and unpaid work. This ultimately depends on restructuring the hours and patterns of employment, for men as well as for women.

The kinds of policies necessary to achieve this range from what is already practised in some social democracies (notably in Scandinavia) to what we can hardly begin to imagine. They would include substantial periods of paid parental leave that could be taken by either mothers or fathers; a requirement on employers to offer reduced working hours to any employees (male or female) who carry major responsibilities for caring for the young, sick or old; additional rights to periods of unpaid leave that would allow people to break their employment without losing their right to their job; and, most important of all, a major reduction in the hours, and alteration in the shifts, of **male** employment, so that male workers are equally enabled to assume their caring responsibilities. To put this more generally, the necessary changes would involve a final, much belated, recognition that the typical worker is no longer a man with a housewife in tow, and a reordering of the priorities of employment to recognise that all of us have a great deal to do outside the factory and office.

Left to its own devices, an unregulated market economy can never deliver this. The market is no great respector of sexual distinction when it comes to employment practices: there has been no wringing of hands over the decline of male employment in the old bases of manufacturing industry and the simultaneous increase in female employment; the market has not stepped in to restore masculine pride. But while we may well rely on the forces of free competition to equalise participation rates between women and men, we cannot rely on these forces to reshape the hours and conditions of work. It is, indeed, one of the appalling ironies of the present period that high levels of unemployment coincide with an extraordinary intensification of work for those lucky enough to find jobs, and that the very insecurities of the job market have exposed people to longer and more unsocial hours. The market will happily release a significant proportion of adults from the constraints of paid employment, but it does this only to doom others to workaholic excess, and we cannot realistically rely on this market to establish sensible divisions between paid employment, care work, and leisure. Only a direct political initiative, underpinned by a strong commitment to sexual equality, could put the necessary changes in place.

Having said that, the kind of socialism required to achieve these changes may not be particularly radical. When Karl Marx examined the struggles in nineteenth century Britain to reduce the length of the working day, he argued that when the restrictions were imposed, they ultimately turned out to capital's advantage. Employers were forced to abandon the rather primitive approach to profits that depended on lengthening the working day, and turn their attention to raising the productivity of labour. (In Marx's terms, they had to switch their efforts from absolute to relative surplus value.) The result was further and often spectacular improvements in profitability - but left to their own devices, the employers would never have agreed to shortening the working day. It took a major political initiative (and as it happened, one that particularly restricted the employment of women workers) to force them into a new round of economic development. Reshaping employment patterns so that they fit with the needs and realities of the labour market might well have similar effects; the kind of sexual equality I outline here might then turn out to be compatible with a capitalist economy. It is not compatible, however, with a hands-off non-interventionism that allows the immediate requirements of employers to dictate the hours and patterns of work.

What I am describing here is more accurately described as social-democracy than socialism, but it does imply a radically different scale of values in which production is tailored to social need, and caring for people takes equal priority alongside producing marketable services and goods. Socialism in this (rather attenuated) sense *is* a precondition for sexual equality, for freeing up the opportunities of girls in education or women in employment does not provide the necessary structural changes that can deliver life-long equality, and we need a more decisive challenge to market principles. It is impossible to eliminate all inequalities between people; it is undesirable to eliminate all differences. But both differences and inequalities have to be detached from the accident of being born male or female, so that the choices we make and the inequalities we condone reflect individual, rather than sexual, variation. It was the liberal tradition that first gave voice to this ideal, but it is socialism that could make it reality.

THE STATE PSYCHOANALYSIS IS IN

Psychoanalysis and the Public Sphere 10th Anniversary Conference

Friday 22nd November 1996, 2.00 - 8.00pm and Saturday 23rd, 10.00 - 5.30pm

Conference Centre, Duncan House, High Street, Stratford, University of East London, London E15

Sponsored by the Free Associations Journal, The Human Nature Trust and the Department of Human Relations, University of East London

Fee: **£75 two days**
£45 one day
£45 concessions

PLEASE APPLY TO THE ADDRESS ABOVE OR, FOR FURTHER INFORMATION, RING JOAN TREMBLE ON 0181 849 3460

Speakers will include:

David P. Levine
Gary Winship
Anthony Elliott
Sue White and
John Stancombe
Phyllis Creme
David Kennard
Ivan Ward
Anna Vidali and
Larry Hirschhorn

Globalisation

Ten frequently asked questions and some surprising answers

Paul Hirst and Grahame Thompson

This article challenges the fashionable view that globalisation has now created a new kind of international economic system.

Globalisation is the greatest threat to the existence of the pragmatic reforming left since 1945. What is at stake can be seen from a recent influential pamphlet by John Gray.[1] He claims that economic globalisation has developed to the point that social democratic policies of national economic regulation and egalitarian redistribution are no longer viable. National governments and organised labour are powerless when faced with international marketisation, neo-liberal de-regulation and global economic integration. These changes are irreversible and social democratic national strategies have become so ineffective that they will have to be scrapped in favour of other methods of meliorating the effects of capitalist markets.

This claim seems plausible, not least because social democratic parties have been politically unsuccessful and conventional strategies of reflationary macro-economic management have proved ineffective. It needs to be firmly resisted. Firstly, because many of the sources of failure of the reformist left have domestic rather than global causes, and because many of the left's problems have been created by the left itself. Secondly, because the notion of globalisation is just plain wrong.

---

1. J Gray, *After Social Democracy*, Demos, London 1996.

The idea of a new, highly-internationalised, virtually uncontrollable global economy based on world market forces has taken root very strongly. It is being used to tell workers and the poor that they must accept whatever is left when their lives and hopes have been sacrificed on the altar of international competitiveness. Fortunately, the story is very different in fact and our options much greater. In what follows we will concentrate on marshalling the evidence to answer ten frequently-asked questions about the world economy and thus show why the rhetoric of the globalisers is wide of the mark. The answers are surprising and we hope that in most cases the surprises are welcome too.

Is globalisation new?

If we interpret globalisation to mean an open international economy with large and growing flows of trade and capital investment between countries, then the answer to the question is clearly negative. The international economy has a complex history of relative openness and closure, since a truly integrated world trading system was created in the second half of the nineteenth century. Submarine telegraph cables from the 1860s onwards connected inter-continental markets. They made possible day-to-day trading and price-making across thousands of miles, a far greater innovation than the advent of electronic trading today. Chicago and London, Melbourne and Manchester were linked in close to real time. Bond markets also became closely inter-connected, and large-scale international lending - both portfolio and direct investment - grew rapidly during this period.

The economy of the *belle époque* from 1870-1914 was remarkably internationalised, and we have only begun to return to those levels of openness today. First we will consider merchandise trade. The key measure is exports and imports combined as a proportion of gross domestic product (GDP). In 1913 the UK's trade was 44.7 per cent of its GDP; after a dramatic fall in the inter-war years, it had risen to 39.3 per cent in 1973 and still had not equalled its pre World War I level in 1993 at 40.5. France and Germany offer a similar picture: France has still not returned to 1913 levels of openness (35.4); in 1973 its ratio stood at 29.0 per cent, in 1993 at 32.4 per cent; for Germany the figures are 1913 35.1 per cent, 1973 35.2 per cent, 1993 38.3 per cent, a modest increase but hardly enough to sustain the notion of massive 'globalisation' in recent years. In Japan's case the figures show a marked *decline* from 31.4 per cent in 1913, to 18.3 per cent in 1973, to 14.4 per cent in 1993.[2] Clearly, Japan has been reducing its imports, but it still exports a relatively low percentage of its GDP - 8.8 per cent in 1991-3, down from a high of 11.8 per cent in 1979-81.[3] For exports alone, we find that Western Europe exported 18.3 per cent of its GDP in 1913, 17.4 per cent in 1970 and 21.7 per cent in 1992; the USA exported 6.4 per cent in 1913, 4 per cent in 1970 and 7.5 per cent in 1992 and Japan 12.5 per cent in 1913, 9.7 per cent in 1970 and 8.8 per cent in 1992.[4] Thus, apart from the increased openness of the USA in both exports and imports since the 1970s, the economies of the major developed countries are not markedly more open in trade-to-GDP ratio terms than they were before 1914 - although the *volume* of trade has increased massively.

Capital mobility was as marked a feature of the *belle époque* international economy as it is of the world economy today. Bairoch and Kozul-Wright comment, for example, that the stock of foreign direct investment (FDI) in 1913 reached over 9 per cent of world output and note that this figure was still not surpassed in the early 1990s.[5] They also point out that between 1870-1913 foreign portfolio investment grew faster than trade, FDI and output. *Plus ça change.* The UK, France and Germany were the major capital exporters - the UK exporting an average of 4 per cent of national income per annum in 1870-1914 and an astounding 9 per cent at the end of the period.

World trade has a complex and chequered history. It was severely damaged by the Great Depression of the 1930s, when countries with high trade-to-GDP ratios like Britain and Germany suffered devastating losses of about 40 per cent in their foreign trade. The open international economy restructured by the *Pax Americana* after 1945 promoted rapid growth in world trade. Between 1950-73 trade grew at an average annual rate of 9.4 per cent as against an average of 5.3 per cent for output. The figures for 1973-84 were 3.6 per cent for trade and 2.1 per cent for output. In the period 1872-1914 trade grew at an average of 3.5 per cent and output at 3.45 per cent.[6] If there was a period of rapid internationalisation it was

---

2. P. Hirst and G. Thompson, 'Global Myths and National Policies', *Renewal* Vol. 4 No. 2 1996, Table 1 p 60 - see also M. Wolf, 'Globalisation and the State', *Financial Times* 18.9.95, p.25.
3. P. Bairoch, 'Globalisation, Myths and Realities' in R. Boyer and D. Drache, *States Against Markets - The Limits of Globalisation,* Routledge, London 1996, Table 7.1, p176.
4. P. Bairoch and R. Kozul-Wright, 'Globalisation Myths: Some Historical Reflections on Integration, Industralisation and Growth in the World Economy', UNCTAS Discussion Paper No. 113, March 1996, Table 1, p6.
5. Bairoch and Kozul-Wright, *op.cit.*, p10.
6. P. Hirst and G. Thompson, *Globalisation in Question,* Polity, Cambridge 1996, Table 2.4, p22.

the managed multi-lateralism of the Keynesian era. Growth in world merchandise trade only returned to the levels of the Great Boom in 1994 at 9.5 per cent (trade grew between 1983-1990 at an average annual rate of 9 per cent).[7]

The more naive advocates of rapid and recent 'globalisation' have short memories and they tend to see the international economy in post 1973 terms. A longer perspective is sobering, not merely for what it reveals about the pre-1914 world economy, but because it shows how volatile, how subject to conjuncture change, and how vulnerable to the effects of political conflict the international economy is. No major regime has lasted for longer than 30-40 years and periods of considerable openness and growth have been replaced by closure and decline. It would be naive, therefore, to project current trends towards openness and integration forward as if they are inevitable or irreversible.

An open international economy is worth preserving. To support free trade against a return to generalised protectionism does not mean that we are thereby tied to all the institutions and circumstances of the present world economy with all its inequalities and unfairness. An unregulated free-market international economy, organised solely for the benefit of the richest nations and largest companies, is unlikely to be socially or environmentally sustainable. Genuine economic openness requires multilateral regulation to prevent unfair competition, to redress the debt burden on the poorest countries, to distribute investment more equitably, and to compensate poorer countries for declining terms of trade. Such a policy requires new priorities on the part of the advanced countries and international institutions like the IMF, the World Bank, and the World Trade Organisation. Alarmist rhetoric about 'globalisation' is counter-productive in this context because it makes people afraid of an open trading economy and more inclined to support protectionism.

Is capital mobility a threat to jobs and living standards? Is capital now chasing low wages?

These questions can be more accurately, if ponderously, be re-phrased thus: Is the new international capital mobility made possible by the de-regulation of financial markets and the removal of exchange controls in major advanced economies in the early 1980s leading to a significant loss of employment and output in the advanced nations as production shifts to exploit the benefits of low wages in the

7. *International Trade Trends and Statistics 1993*, World Trade Organisation 1995, Table 1.5, p7.

newly industrialising countries (NICs)?

This is a fear that unites sections of the left and the populist right. For example, prior to the conclusion of the North American Free Trade Agreement, both sections of the US trade union movement and Ross Perot argued that it would result in a massive loss of jobs in the USA as firms shifted south of the Mexican border to exploit low wages.

The evidence flatly contradicts the notion of a massive flight of capital from the advanced nations to low-wage countries in the Third World since the early 1980s. In 1993 capital flows from advanced nations to the NICs totalled over $100 billion. Surely this staggering figure must represent a massive loss of potential investment? One of the great bugbears of 'globalisation' talk is the quoting of apparently large numbers out of context. As Paul Krugman points out the combined GNP of North America, Western Europe and Japan (the Triad) in 1993 was $18 trillion, their investment $3.5 trillion and their capital stock about $60 trillion: $100 billion thus represents 3 per cent of investment in the rich Triad countries and 0.2 per cent of their capital stocks.[8] He calculates that between 1990-93, the boom in investment in Third World markets reduced the stock of capital of the advanced world by 0.5 per cent.

Even if such foreign investment had no other effect than *reducing* Western employment and output, the figures are just not big enough to generate the kind of panic one currently sees in the West. Given the pitiful levels of foreign aid provided by most rich countries, these transfers of capital could be seen as a modest contribution to reducing the vast disparities in wealth and industrial output between the First and Third Worlds. Foreign direct investment in Third World countries is not necessarily negative for western workers, it may also create demand for western goods by promoting output and national income elsewhere - just as Britain's foreign investment generated expanded commerce with the exports to countries like Argentina and Uruguay before 1914.

Job losses and unemployment in the advanced world are just too big to be explained by trade with low-wage countries. It has been calculated that if the USA had enjoyed balanced trade in manufactured goods rather than a large deficit, the decline in manufacturing as a share of GDP between 1970-1990 would have been from 24.9 per cent to 19.2 per cent - the actual figure was from 25 per cent to

---

8. Paul Krugman, *Pop Internationalism*, MIT Press, Cambridge MA 1996, p63.

18.4 per cent.[9] The USA became a far more open economy after 1970, suffering massive import penetration, mainly from advanced economies like Japan. If a relatively small part of US job losses is represented by import penetration, then a tiny fraction of those losses in turn are due to Third World imports of manufactured goods. Manufacturing exports from low-wage countries are only a small part of the market for manufactured goods in the advanced countries: 4.3 per cent in the USA in the second half of the 1980s, approximately 3 per cent in the major EU countries and 2.6 per cent in Japan.[10] The main causes of job losses are domestic to the advanced countries.

Foreign direct investment (FDI) has since the early 1980s been growing at over 3.5 times the rate of merchandise trade (1983-1990 34 per cent pa v 9 per cent p.a.). FDI is an alternative to trade in manufactures; it creates branch plants and assembly operations, and it is also the main way in which countries can 'export' marketed services, such as hotels or retailing. FDI and trade remain massively concentrated within the advanced countries. Closer integration is above all between the three major blocs of the Triad. In 1992, including inter-EU trade, the Triad represented 70 per cent of world trade and, excluding inter-European trade, the figure was still 60 per cent. The ten most important recipients of FDI among the developing countries represented 18.2 per cent of total world trade (excluding inter-EU trade). In the case of FDI flows, between 1981-91 North America, Western Europe and Japan represented 75 per cent of the total. The Triad's members invest mainly in each other and in other advanced countries. The ten major developing country recipients of FDI absorbed 16.5 per cent of the total flows during this period; representing with the Triad 91.5 per cent of total FDI. In population terms the Triad, the nine most important developing countries in respect of FDI, and the eight coastal provinces of China, plus Beijing, are 28 per cent of the world's population. This leaves the other 72 per cent, most of whom are very poor, with less than 10 per cent of total FDI.[11] If FDI is changing the world it is to make the rich richer, and to propel a small number of developing countries, like Taiwan, close to advanced country status.

In the developing world foreign direct investment is highly concentrated. Of the total of \$126.1 billion of FDI going to the ten largest recipients in 1988-92,

---

9. Krugman, *op. cit.*, p36.
10. A. Glynn, 'The Assessment: Unemployment and Inequality', *Oxford Review of Economic Policy,* Vol. 11 No. 1995, pp1-25.
11. Hirst and Thompson, *Globalisation in Question,* Tables 3.2 and 3.3, pp 68-69.

$47.3 billion went to just two countries - China and Singapore - and $78 billion (or roughly two -thirds of the total) went to just four countries.[12] Africa and the poorest countries in Asia like Bangladesh have been all but excluded from the 1990s boom in FDI. Moreover, the figures for investment do not just represent western firms investing in low-wage manufacturing sectors abroad. Foreign investment in China has surged from around $5 billion per annum in 1990 to over $25 billion in 1993. But the IMF notes that much of FDI comes not from the West but from near neighbours (Hong Kong, Macau and Taiwan), that it is highly concentrated in the coastal provinces, and that it is highly concentrated in certain sectors like real estate and natural resources.[13]

If Western capitalists are moving capital abroad to take advantage of low wages in order to produce cheap manufactured goods in order to export them to the West, then they are making a bad job of it.

Is Third World competition destroying First World jobs? Must wages in newly industrialised countries remain low?

Alarmists are not just concerned by capital mobility but by Third World industrialisation in general. Countries like South Korea and Taiwan have industrialised primarily by domestic capital formation, rather than by high levels of FDI or international borrowing. The fear is that Third World newly industrialising countries will be able to exploit low wages to gain competitive edge and penetrate western markets, and that a combination of relatively well-educated workers and technology transfer will enable them to match western quality in manufacturers. The result will be a collapse of manufacturing employment and output in the West.

But how is this scenario possible? Falling output and employment would restrict demand in the West, and a loss of tradable manufacturing goods would restrict the advanced countries' ability to trade. Trade is not like inter-company competition. If company A outsells company B and drives it to bankruptcy that is the end of the matter. But international trade requires some rough approximation of *balance* overall; other things being equal, a country must have goods it can trade with others if it is to continue to import. Manufactured goods are central to trade between the advanced countries and also a key component of their trade with the developing world. Low-wage exporters can

12. *Economist*,1 October 1994, p29.
13. *World Economic Outlook*, IMF, October 1994, p52.

only displace this trade if Western countries find other things to make and sell abroad. Exporters who are highly competitive but have low domestic demand because of low home-country wages can only exist in particular niches. If they came to dominate trade in manufactures then world markets would begin to collapse. Some elementary trade theory and macro-economics will show why. Output and employment are falling in the advanced countries. Output is rising in the low-wage exporters but not domestic demand. Trade will not balance and there will be a massive shortage of effective demand. This is madhouse economics on a world scale and need not be taken seriously.

The only sustainable option for international trade is the win-win outcome, in which rising output and employment in newly industrialising countries lead to rapid growth and rising real incomes, with growing markets for Western goods. Of course, certain sectors are displaced in the advanced countries and others face intensified competition and therefore have to improve productivity and innovation. Thus western countries continue to have a range of goods to trade internationally, and emerging markets in which to sell them. This may seem optimistic, covering over a good deal of possible dislocation and job losses, but in the end trade is driven by the crude logic that countries must have goods that others want.

Moreover, there is evidence that the most successful newly industrialising countries are experiencing rapid growth faster in South Korea than in any advanced industrial country - in 1979-83 21.6 per cent, 1983-84 39.5 per cent, 1987-89 73.1 per cent and total growth over the period 1979-89 of 193.7 per cent. The comparable rates of growth in the UK and Japan over the same period were 88.2 per cent and 71.4 per cent respectively.[14] This is of course growth from a very low base, but the following table shows the likely outcome of Korea's successful industrialisation and its rising incomes on its cost structure.

Table 1:   Extrapolated total labour costs per employee 1989-99 in $US

	France	Germany	Italy	UK	US	Japan	S. Korea
1989	29,423	31,857	28,630	21,301	30,829	30,963	12,464
1999	37,600	47,785	59,006	40,088	44,918	53,071	36,607

Source: Thompson (1995) Table 2, p103

14. G. Thompson, 'A Comment on "The Crisis of Cost Recovery and the Waste of the Industrialised Nations', *Competition and Change* Vol. 1, 1995, pp 101-110.

This is a relatively crude extrapolation from rates of change that could easily alter, but it makes the point that South Korea could be nearly as expensive a producer as France and the UK early in the 21st century. It will thus have to follow a variant of the Japanese path, a route made harder by the fact that its home market is much smaller than Japan's (44 million against 124 million people in 1992). Japan has had a favourable balance of trade for a considerable time, but its exports are a small percentage of GDP. The greater part of Japan's output is consumed domestically.

Countries like Singapore and Hong Kong are seen as economic miracles in the West and silly politicians imagine that they are the new 'models' for the 21st century, but there is little that is surprising in their economic success. Both are entrepôts with high ratios of re-exports to exports in merchandise trade. Singapore exported $58.3 billion of domestic goods in 1994 and re-exported $38.5 billion and Hong Kong exported $28.7 billion of domestic goods in 1994 and re-exported $122.7 billion. In both cases domestic imports at $64.2 billion and $43.2 billion respectively were greater than domestic exports.[15] Neither conforms to the high-export, low-import, low-wage producer that some western politicians and commentators fear. But western 'Tiger watchers' are afraid of an almost impossible entity; the economic equivalent of the frictionless machine.

Do multinationals now dominate world output and trade? Are such companies becoming trans-national and ceasing to have national loyalties?

Many people are concerned that a globalised economy means the dominance of uncontrollable world market forces and that multi-national companies will become the dominant actors in such markets, having escaped from the scope of national regulation. Such firms will locate wherever economic advantage dictates. They will seek to dump costs on local governments and taxpayers, they will threaten to move if challenged, and they will seek to drive down both wages and social overhead costs.

Multinational companies can be defined as those with subsidiaries and affiliates in more than one national jurisdiction. The question is whether output and employment in the internationally-traded sectors of the world economy and in the major industrialised nations is becoming dominated by such companies. The

---

15. *International Trade Trends and Statistics*, 1993, WTO 1995, Table 1.7, p13.

have prejudices; they favour low inflation, 'sound money' public policies. There is little conflict with national governments of the major industrial powers here because most central bankers and national economic policy makers think the same way. These policies undoubtedly inhibit growth and they establish the short-term interest of major financial institutions as the supreme economic wisdom.

This is not a satisfactory situation. The advanced world is trading jobs and growth for low inflation - the price is the growth of unemployment and poverty in the major industrial nations. But this is not quite the disaster of volatile casino-like financial markets wrecking real economies that the most alarmist counsels of the danger of unregulated international markets claim. Moreover, the markets are no longer *that* volatile or unregulated - they are probably governed just about enough to prevent meltdown. After the break-up of the Bretton Woods system in the early 1970s and the 1973 and 1979 oil price hikes, there was a period of floating and highly volatile exchange rates. The turbulence was gradually brought under control; with the Plaza accord of 1985 and the Louvre Accord of 1987 governments restored some minimal stability to the international monetary system. Throughout the 1980s, the dismantling of exchange controls has been accompanied by the re-regulation of financial institutions and markets through the Bank of International Settlements and other agencies. This sets the rules for such activities but does not attempt to steer or alter the price-making functions of markets.[20]

This is not enough, but it shows that governance is possible. The vast majority of actors in the financial markets have an interest in a minimum degree of calculability in the international system too - not just exporters and long-term international investors. Incalculable risks undermine expectations, and thus extreme volatility is a growth and investment killer. Markets and institutions accept this for the turbulence caused by high inflation; they need to be made to realise that the turbulence created by exchange-rate crises will do this, but attitudes are slowly changing. Most international trading is done by major financial institutions that have definite expectations to meet - those of pensioners, bulk depositors, maturing policy holders, and not least, those of their own shareholders for dividends. They have used the markets to make profits on short-term dealing and to hedge against risk. The Barings and Sumitomo scandals

---

20. Hirst and Thompson, *Globalisation in Question*, Ch. 6, pp129-36.

may well force the senior managements of the major institutions to seek greater regulation within their companies and also greater regulations of the major international markets. In the long run the markets will only be further re-regulated if the major actors in them see the benefits of doing so or if a combination of powerful governments decides to act in a co-ordinated way. At present neither of these things is likely. The world financial markets are not inherently ungovernable. The problem is the will to govern them, not the want of means. Given the will there is a variety of possible options, like James Tobin's turnover tax on short-term international financial movements.

Will globalisation drive down both wages and welfare provision in the advanced countries?

Again this needs to be re-phrased somewhat more ponderously, as follows: do wages, levels of welfare provision and rations of public spending to GDP in the advanced nations have to converge to the lowest possible level as a result of competition between them and with the developing nations to attract and retain capital?

Consider wages first. There is some evidence that for unskilled wages in manufacturing Third World competition does have a depressive effect. This is strongly argued by Adrian Wood.[21] However, in most major economies in the developed world, such low-wage manufacturing sectors are not large enough to affect overall wages for the unskilled - most of whom work in low-productivity service jobs in sectors that are not internationally tradable. In the case of the USA imports from low wage countries (less than 50 per cent US wage levels) were a mere 2.8 per cent of GDP - far too little to affect overall wage rates significantly.[22] Trying to compete with the Third World in wage costs in manufacturing is impossible - from China to Indonesia workers are available at a tiny fraction of the hourly rate for western manufacturing employees whether skilled or unskilled.

Cutting wage costs may restore comparative advantage against other comparable advanced country producers, offsetting productivity differentials. The UK has recently followed a strategy of wage-cutting and competitive devaluation,

---

21. A. Wood, 'How Trade Hurt Unskilled Workers', *Journal of Economic Perspectives*, Vol. 9 No. 3, Summer 1995, pp57-80 and A. Wood, *North-South Trade, Employment and Inequality - Changing Fortunes in a Skill-Driven World*, Clarendon Press, Oxford 1994.
22. Krugman, *op. cit.*, p47.

mainly against its European Union partners. This is a short-term strategy that might make some sense if the UK were at the same time attempting to address by other means the problem of differential productivity. But, if it becomes a substitute for sustained productivity enhancement (and in the UK's case it seems to be) then it locks the country in question on a low-wage path and into having to export a larger proportion of its output to match imports. It appears that wages are not being greatly depressed by Third World competition and that the strategy of low-wage competition against other advanced countries is not sustainable in the long term except at the price of falling ever further behind in relative standards of living.

'The low-wage strategy is best described as seeking competitive advantage by sweating'

This does not stop illiterate politicians and ideologically-crazed economists claiming that the UK will become more 'competitive' if the wages of British office cleaners are reduced to starvation levels. How they are 'competing' with their equivalents in Jakarta or Shanghai is not clear, since most unskilled services will never be internationally tradable. This low-wage strategy is best described as seeking competitive advantage by sweating - but it is mad. In the tradable sector we cannot compete on wages with very low-wage countries - what are we going to pay? 50p or 30p an hour? In the non-tradable sector trying to force down unskilled wages to poverty levels will mainly have the effect of shifting income from labour to profits. Moreover, a generalised strategy of wage-cutting will depress domestic effective demand, output and employment. Public officials who believe they are 'saving' public money by such strategies ought to be sacked; ultimately they are undermining the national economy to line the pockets of bottom-of-the-bucket cheapskate employers. The sources of such policies are not 'global' pressures, but a mixture of domestic interest groups using this rhetoric to feather their own nests and a failure of nerve by those who should be offering clear alternative policies, a timidity reinforced by the belief in global competitive threats. Radical reflationary policies face serious domestic constraints at the moment, but that is no reason to further inhibit domestic performance by self-defeating attitudes on wages and working conditions.[23]

---

23. See Hirst and Thompson, 'Global Myths and National Policies', for an attempt to spell out why these constraints are domestic.

Many globalisers see current European levels of welfare and public expenditure to GDP ratios as unsustainable. Robert Skidelsky argues, for example, that public expenditure ratios need to be pushed back to the 30 per cent of GDP that they were in most cases in the 1960s.[24] Andrew Marr contends that high ratios of public spending to national income are a reflection of economic failure and unemployment.[25] The state will have to tax and spend less in the long run; it will have to take the medicine imposed by global competitive pressures or face capital flight.

Such arguments are not supported by either economic theory or evidence. Why 30 per cent, why not 10 per cent or 48 per cent? Who says current levels of public expenditure in Europe are unsustainable? The *Economist*, not noted for its opposition to the notion of globalisation, recognises that there are wide and persisting variations in the percentage of GDP devoted to public spending - in 1994, 20 per cent in Singapore, 33 per cent in the USA, 49 per cent in Germany and 68 per cent in Sweden.[26] Table 2 gives comparative data on government expenditures as a percentage of GDP. All the countries listed show a growth in the ratio, despite, in the case of the UK and USA, attempts to cut government expenditure in the 1980s.

Table 2:	General Government Total Expenditure 1960-1995 (% GDP at market prices)				
	1960	1970	1980	1990	1995
Austria	35.6	39.2	48.8	49.3	52.7
France	34.6	38.9	46.6	50.5	54.1
W. Germany	32.5	38.5	48.0	45.3	49.1*
Italy	30.1	34.2	41.9	53.2	53.5
Japan	n/a	19.4	32.6	32.3	34.9
Sweden	n/a	43.7	61.2	60.7	69.4
UK	32.2	37.3	43.2	40.3	42.5
USA	27.0	31.6	33.7	36.7	36.1

*Notes: * - United Germany; Source: European Economy No. 60 (1996)*
Derived from Table 61, pp212-213

24. R. Skidelsky, *The World After Communism*, Macmillan, London 1995; and 'Welfare without the State', *Prospect*, January 1996, pp 38-43.
25. Andrew Marr, 'Stuck between the flab and a hard place', *Independent* ,19.10.95; and A. Marr, *Ruling Britannia* , Penguin Books, 1996, Ch. 6.
26. 'The Myth of the Powerless State', *Economist*, 7.10.1995.

The data also shows persistent differences in ratios of government expenditures to GDP between states over the last twenty five years. Austria has been at the high end and the USA at the bottom end throughout, for example. Moreover, there has been no consistent effect on growth rates. Thus Japan and the USA both have low GDP ratios for public expenditure but very different rates of growth. Slemrod (1995) in a thorough survey of the relationships between taxation and government expenditure on the one hand and GDP growth rates and prosperity on the other, found no systematic or robust empirical relationship between high government expenditure and poor economic performance.[27] This is not so say there is *no* level of public expenditure to GDP that would not be growth-inhibiting, but that the opponents of the current levels have yet to make a coherent case for such a general effect.

Moreover, it is by no means clear that public expenditures are driven primarily by welfare spending or that such spending varies markedly overtime or that current levels are unsustainable. The table on the following page measures social protection - health, pensions, unemployment benefits and other income support - it shows considerable stability rather than relentless and insupportable growth.

If this is the case, why is there so much concern about social spending? In part because governments in the bulk of the advanced world have been running more or less substantial budgetary deficits and social expenditures seem easier to freeze and cut than some other programmes. The figure of 3 per cent of GDP as a desirable upper limit for government net borrowing in the Maastricht criteria for EMU is exerting a clear depressive pressure on government expenditures in the EU. It certainly helps to try to justify the cuts thus imposed by appealing to the needs of international competitiveness, even if the real reason is the consequence of seeking to make economies with divergent performances converge in order to pursue the goal of monetary union with low inflation. Government receipts have fallen relative to expenditure in many countries. In some cases this is a result of tax-cutting strategies, or because of poor macro-economic management and miscalculations about the timing and strength of economic recoveries. But these are domestic choices and policy errors by national economic managers, not the relentless and direct pressure of global markets. Provided a country remains competitive in the goods and services it trades

---

27. J. Slemrod, 'What do Cross-Country Studies Teach about Government Involvement, Prosperity and Economic Growth', Brookings Papers on Economic Activity 2, 1995, pp373-431.

internationally, it can still choose high levels of social spending and collective consumption. There is no clear evidence that public expenditure *per se* undermines growth or economic performance.

Table 3:   Total Public Expenditure on Social Protection (% of GDP)

	1980	1981	1982	1983	1984	1985	1986	1987	1988	1989	1990
EC COUNTRIES											
Belgium	25.4	27.4	28.1	28.4	27.9	27.5	27.2	26.6	25.2	25.2	25.2
Denmark	26.0	27.6	28.1	28.0	26.8	26.0	24.8	25.7	27.8	27.8	27.8
France	23.9	25.4	26.5	27.3	27.8	27.9	27.4	27.0	26.4	26.4	26.5
Germany	25.4	26.3	26.6	25.8	25.4	25.2	24.7	25.0	24.1	24.1	23.5
Greece	13.4	14.9	17.9	18.4	19.1	20.1	20.6	20.8	20.9	20.9	*
Ireland	20.6	21.1	22.5	23.5	23.0	23.1	23.3	22.5	19.6	19.6	19.7
Italy	19.8	20.8	21.5	23.0	22.2	22.7	22.5	23.2	23.7	23.7	24.5
Luxembourg	26.0	27.2	26.4	26.0	25.0	25.0	24.4	25.9	26.6	26.6	27.3
Netherlands	27.2	28.4	30.2	30.8	29.7	28.8	28.4	29.0	27.9	27.9	28.8
Portugal	13.6	15.2	14.1	13.6	13.6	13.8	14.3	14.9	14.9	14.9	15.3
Spain	16.8	17.9	18.0	18.7	18.5	19.0	18.4	18.2	18.8	18.8	19.3
United Kingdom	21.3	23.3	23.6	24.0	24.0	24.1	23.9	22.9	21.9	21.3	22.3
	1980	1981	1982	1983	1984	1985	1986	1987	1988	1989	1990
EFTA COUNTRIES											
Austria	23.4	24.2	24.1	24.4	24.4	24.8	25.1	25.4	25.3	25.1	24.5
Finland	21.4	22.1	23.3	24.2	24.6	25.9	26.3	26.7	25.6	25.4	27.1
Norway	21.4	22.0	22.5	23.0	23.0	22.1	24.2	26.2	27.0	28.1	28.7
Sweden	32.4	33.3	33.5	33.8	32.7	32.6	33.9	33.5	34.1	33.3	33.1
	1980	1981	1982	1983	1984	1985	1986	1987	1988	1989	1990
NORTH AMERICA											
Canada	*	*	17.3	17.5	17.1	17.1	17.7	17.4	17.0	17.2	18.8
United States	14.1	14.3	15.0	15.3	14.3	14.3	14.4	14.4	14.4	14.5	14.6

* - data not available
Source: OECD Social Protection database Table 4.7 p151
OECD Employment Outlook July 1994

Is the world economy now ungovernable and must global market forces inevitably overwhelm and subvert distinctive national projects of governance?

It should be clear by now that globalisation has not swept away national economies. The political and business elites of advanced western nations have found globalisation a convenient cloak for the domestic policies they have chosen to follow - especially in the UK and USA. There are many reasons why full employment is difficult to attain, why social solidarity and social welfare are under severe pressure, why electorates are tax-averse, and why organised labour has much less power than it once did. But these changes are common to the social structures of many advanced societies and are not primarily the consequence of international competitive pressures. It is equally true that, while a great deal can be accomplished by national policies for economic management and social renewal, the national is merely one level in a complex division of economic and social governance.

Regional and local government has become more salient as industry has become more diversified and has moved away from the Fordist norm of large-scale standardised mass production. Those societies that have exploited the new trends best are those in which national and sub-national governments have achieved, whether deliberately or by happenstance, an appropriate division of labour. Equally, national governance is not in itself adequate for economic management; co-ordinated national action, and international agencies and regimes, are crucial for control of the world economy. This is not new. After 1945 effective national economic management in the advanced countries rested on a firm framework of international institutions underpinned by US hegemony. The true era of 'national' policies, the 1930s, was one of trade crises, bitter rivalry, economic depression and militarism.

The need for regulation of market economies at national level and the requirement for an appropriate system of management of the international economy are linked. Globalisers try to convince us that the international economy is inherently ungovernable and that it is absorbing and subsuming national economies; projects of regulation are thus futile. This is just not true, but national governance does require an effective international framework and the advanced nations must cooperate to provide it. The central problem here is not global markets but divergent *national* interests - those of the USA, Japan, and the major European states. These differences are exacerbated by the fear of global competition and the belief that co-operation is hopeless given the power of the markets. The rhetoric of competitiveness makes people scared, afraid of their own failure, and, therefore, indifferent to the fate of the poor in their own countries and in the Third World. Counterposing the declining role of national sovereignty and the growing salience of international markets and global problems is not useful - modern problems can only be coped with by a complex division of labour in governance. Clinging to 'national sovereignty' is not effective either - national governments are effective only when they cooperate with effective sub-national and supra-national governing powers with a definite sphere of autonomy. If we can work towards such an extended division of labour in governance, if we can reduce fear that economies and societies are beyond control, then peoples and elites in the advanced countries may be willing to pursue more generous and egalitarian policies nationally and internationally.

What might those policies be? First, consider the level of international economic governance, where a great deal more could be accomplished by the economic great powers of the G7 and major international institutions like the World Bank and IMF. A less cautious and more expansionary policy pursued across the advanced world might begin to reduce unemployment and increase the rate of growth. A co-ordinated policy would leave the financial markets less room to impede policies they fear, given their instinctive preference for low inflation rather than growth. This would need to be reinforced by greater regulation of the markets to render short-term movements less profitable and to reduce volatility and rogue trading. A growth-oriented policy in the advanced countries needs to be coupled with a determined attempt to reduce debt for the poorest countries, to increase aid and to distribute foreign direct investment more widely - by tax incentives and levies that steer firms away from the top ten developing countries towards some of the poorer ones. Such policies could be achieved in the near future by more active and co-ordinated policies on the part of the advanced states - what stands in the way is not globalisation but perceptions of 'national interest' by key elites.

At the national level in the advanced countries radical go-it-alone expansionary policies are unlikely to succeed - not just because international markets may disapprove but primarily because, in a changed economic conjuncture, stimulus to demand does not lead to the major and rapid falls in unemployment that Keynes anticipated in the 1930s; most jobs require investment. However that does not mean that countries have to run actively deflationary policies. Equally, in a period of relatively low growth and strong demands on public welfare, it is difficult dramatically to increase levels of public spending. This does not mean that current levels of public expenditure are unsustainable or that existing welfare provision in unsupportable. In Europe the conditions for monetary union under the Maastricht Treaty are deflationary. Perhaps this means that we should slow-down the process of monetary union because of the danger that the cuts required to implement it will damage the European Union *politically* with key constituencies in a number of major member states.

At the regional level new forms of economic governance have been emerging in recent decades, spurred on by the shift from standardised mass production to more customised and quality-oriented manufacturing and services - such diversity has favoured localisation, it has also put a premium on intimate knowledge in the governance of economic sectors and, therefore, emphasised distinctive regional rather than uniform national industrial policies. The effect of this is to favour those countries where well-developed industrial districts are coupled with effective local and regional governments able to provide support and collective services for industry. Highly-centralised states like the UK are at a disadvantage in this respect. The future for governing the economy lies with a division of labour and co-ordination between the international, national and regional levels. States have always been most effective when they have operated in an appropriate context of international institutions and policies - like the managed multilateralism after 1945. The myth of globalisation works to undermine the very notion of such a division of labour, it tells us that the international economy is ungovernable and that national governments are ineffective. That is why it needs to be resisted and refuted.

Pictures at an exhibition

Richard Minns interviews Liudmila Vasileva, a Russian born artist living and working in Bulgaria.

Introduction

Bulgaria is a country situated between Serbia, Macedonia, Romania, Turkey and Greece, with the river Danube to the north, the Black Sea to the east and the Rhodopean mountains to the south next to the Greek border. It is at the heart of the Balkan peninsula, a country which has provided a trade route between the middle-east and the west for centuries and which at various times has also included parts of Greece, Macedonia, Albania and other parts of what was Yugoslavia. Historically it has had very close economic and political links with the former Soviet Union. In the capital, Sofia, there is an imposing church (Alexander Nevsky). It was built earlier this century to commemorate the 200,000 Russian soldiers who died in the liberation of Bulgaria from the Turks in the 1870s. Bulgaria was known in Russia as 'little brother Bulgaria'.

Such close links are being broken but their replacement by alternatives is the cause of much speculation and difficulty. Socialism is now a dirty word. The return of socialists at central and local government level since 1994 seems to prove nothing about the virtues of a particular ideology or programme, only a frustration with changes. Pensions have been decimated, unemployment appears as a new and frightening concept, interest rates were hiked overnight from 67 to 108 per cent in May 1996 as the local currency fell through the floor hour by hour, and ordinary people tell me how much they want to leave their country. In fact the population has declined by one million since 1990 through mass exodus, and the abortion rate is the highest in the region.

The capital is now full of huge Cherokee and Suzuki jeeps, gleaming Mercedes Benz and BMWs, all with their tinted windows cruising up and down the central Vitosha Boulevard. Many are driven by 'big necks' or mafiosi-type characters with their ubiquitous mobile phones. Sometimes it seems that there are more Mercedes cars per head of the population in Sofia than in Berlin - but alongside some dire poverty. Crime has soared. A panel of senior economists has described the country as moving from 'Communism' (supposedly) to 'criminism'. Robberies and blackmail are accompanied in the press by news of bank failures and corruption. The head of the IMF mission to Bulgaria, visiting in May to press for more restructuring and liquidations, had her bag stolen in a leading restaurant.

Cynicism about socialism and disillusionment about the apparent chaos that has taken its place is all around you. But Bulgarians stare with incredulity when I mention that people live in cardboard boxes and shop doorways in the capital of Britain.

Recently I came across an art exhibition in Sofia by an artist from a town called Smolian in the southern Rhodopean mountains. These mountains separate the Aegean Sea from the Thracian plain of central Bulgaria. The plain opens on to the Black Sea coast to the east and Sofia in the west, continuing up to Macedonia and Serbia. Smolian itself is the 'longest town in Bulgaria' stretching along the river Cherna, with a huge old industrial area now characterised by empty sheds and piles of scrap resulting from the collapse of guaranteed Russian markets. The mountain scenery is stunning, marred perhaps by blocks of living 'complexes'.

The artist and designer, Liudmila Vasileva, ironically a Russian emigré, produces beautiful paintings of the area. I talked to her at her exhibition in Sofia and at her studio in Smolian. We talked about her art, about uncertainties caused by economic and social changes, about what we both describe as socialism and capitalism. I felt that many of us would share some of her views although we come from vastly different backgrounds.

The exhibition was called *Through the Window of the Soul* and was open from 20 May to 3 June 1996 at the central architectural centre in Sofia. Fifty paintings were displayed. The opening of the exhibition was filmed by Bulgarian television and appeared on the evening news. In June the exhibition was moved, appropriately enough, to the Russian Embassy.

Liudmila, you spent most of your life in Russia. Why did you come to Bulgaria, a small Balkan country and what do you think of life here?
First of all my English is not too good so I rely on you to help me when you present this interview. You asked me about my background. I came here in 1987 from Petersburg (Leningrad as it was) because I married a Bulgarian and we were going to work together, he a sculptor and me a painter. I now live with my three children in a small apartment in one of the living complexes you can see in Smolian. I am a designer, painter and architect, an architect by profession really, but there is no work, so I have to paint to make a living. I would love sometime to go back to Russia, because I so love Petersburg.

'We've all been let down bitterly by the stupidities of what we were told was Communism, but now there's nothing'

We've all been let down bitterly by the stupidities of what we were told was Communism, but now there's nothing. We were told that capitalism was dead or dying and smelt like a rotting corpse. But the joke was that people would see Western tourists in Moscow or Leningrad and say that they didn't smell so bad for rotting corpses. But now we've lost any social idealism. Anybody who believes in 'society' or 'socialism', 'idealism', as opposed to themselves, is regarded as a fool. 'Look what happened before,' people say, 'when so-called believers in "society" just blossomed and looked after themselves, while we - the real "society" - got nothing'. Socialist planning was not about planning but about making declarations. I think what we need are more 'fools' - people who believe in society, a social ideal, more naivety, romantic idealism. But how? What we have now is an individualism where no-one sees themselves as representing a social interest because that means communism, and we can't have all that again, now can we? I think it's impossible to have idealists

Moika, St Petersburg, a sketch by Liudmila Vasileva

A leaflet advertising Liudmila's exhibition

СЪЮЗЪТ НА АРХИТЕКТИТЕ В БЪЛГАРИЯ
И
КЛУБ "АРХИТЕКТ - ХУДОЖНИК" ПРИ САБ

ВИ КАНЯТ НА
ИЗЛОЖБА

"ПРЕЗ ПРОЗОРЕЦА НА ДУШАТА"

масло • акварел • графика
ЛЮДМИЛА ВАСИЛЕВА

20 май - 3 юни 1996 г.

Откриване на 20 май 1996 г. - 17^{30} часа
Централен дом на архитекта, Зала 2
София ул. "Кракра" 11

now because the way to the top changes people.

Most people are fixated by consumerism. All they talk about is what they've bought or would like to buy. All for what? It's easy to live without love but difficult to love.

But that's not unique to this part of the world, surely? We have cuts in social welfare in the West, and we also have consumer societies. The 'left' has become more consumer biased in an attempt to borrow individualism from the 'right'. No-one talks about socialism any more. In fact there's not much discussion of alternatives at all.

OK, but I don't really understand words like 'left' and 'right'. Maybe it would be easier if I did. I find it quite funny that you use these words. I see things more in terms of trying to achieve a balance or harmony in society as well as in yourself and what you do - like painting for me. It's a personal as well as a social thing. All we've had for decades is self-interest disguised by lies. First it's socialism, now it's something else which is difficult to describe. It's like a theatre. The play's the same, same actors, same script, same audience clapping in the right places, everyone killing time it seems. No individual personalities. It's not surprising. People here have been battered by ideologies for centuries, including the oppression by the Turks for five centuries. You've never seen anything like that. Most people like you enter this country through the main entrance and see the facade. It's important to see it from within.

But I think what we are seeing now is very dangerous both for your country and for this part of the world. Capitalist societies are also vulnerable because of lack of balance. What I mean is that welfare states and socialist revolutions occurred because of lack of balance: welfare states because of the threat of socialism, socialist revolutions because of lack of welfare. Two opposing blocs grew up - capitalism and socialism. Now we've got rid of these opposing blocs and capitalism no longer has to show its 'good side', its balance. We could now see the birth of something else. You can see the need for it. There are so many people here who are just so very poor. I mean really poor. They depend on their children, not the state. But we need new ideas, not more institutions.

Balance is about human nature and the different definitions of it. Capitalism assumes human beings are wild animals, and socialism assumes magnificence. There's probably truth in both but it's a matter of circumstance and creating harmony for individuals and society.

Personally I don't know whether I'm on the left or right, as you describe it. It's meaningless to me. I suppose I'm in favour of creativity, of difference, but that's probably because of an artistic family background, where my grandfather was a writer and my father an artist. Whether it's the west or the east it's the same when societies kill creativity, or make it dependent on conformity or politics. Or social circumstances like in small communities here in Bulgaria where to be different is to be an outcast. A person should be able to occupy free space - and countries and communities can be chains or ties. That's how I feel personally, especially being a Russian and a female by herself here. I'm not being negative, just realistic.

What about your work?
I paint the mountains and valleys around in the Smolian region. They're beautiful. You know, there's a myth about the woman of the Rhodopean mountains which I try to capture in some of my work. She ran away from some god like Zeus who was after lots of women and she changed into the mountains to escape him. The mountains are now like the body of a woman. You can see some of the pictures of her here at the exhibition.

The region is also full of history and legends like the story of Orpheus and Eurydice who are supposed to come from the area. I try to show how haunting the mountains are. It's also reflected in traditional Rhodopean music which has to be heard to be believed. The mountains also contain tragedy. There is a huge crag outside Smolian called 'Neviastata', literally 'Young woman'. This refers to the many young women who jumped off the mountain during Turkish rule, not wanting to be sent to the harem. They would tie their hair together so that no-one could change her mind when the first jumped.

I also have paintings here at the exhibition that I did of Petersburg when I was living there.

I sell my paintings to local companies and banks, and to bar owners and restaurants, also to visitors like you. I also depend on exhibitions like this. As well I do design work. I enter international competitions to try and get some extra money and recognition. I have also just done a diploma in economics because I want to develop some ideas for greater links between art and culture here, and possibilities for displaying more of this in the west. There are so many people in the region involved in painting, sculpture, pottery, music, all sorts of creative activity. In the end it comes down to us to do something about it and our future.

Pictures from the exhibition

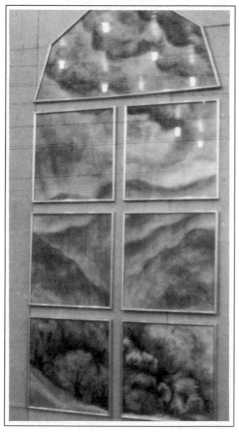

In Smolian we have a beautiful library where I have my studio, and a museum and art gallery. The set of buildings was designed by a woman architect and they are much more in harmony with the mountains than most. They are built at different levels. But they sit there - their potential could be much greater. The museum is falling to bits.

You mentioned your father and grandfather.

My grandfather, Mihail Bubennov, was a writer. He volunteered to join the Soviet army in the second world war and, in his spare time, wrote a book about the war called *The White Birch*. It was very difficult. There was hardly any spare time because the war in Russia was full-time, all-absorbing, and many of his close friends were killed. Anyway, there's an amusing story that my father told me about when Stalin read my grandfather's book. I don't know how true it is. After the war it was very difficult to write books about it because you would be afraid of saying something not correct according to socialism. My grandfather wrote the story as a romance and it was published in the *Moscow Journal*. Stalin read it. One night a big black car pulled up outside my grandfather's apartment and he was driven away, he didn't know where. He was taken to see Stalin who told him how much he liked his writing. All this took place in the middle of the night, as was Stalin's habit. Stalin didn't know that my grandfather was not in the Communist Party. Eventually he was given a major prize by Stalin and was made famous. He was very ill because of the war but then got the best medical care. But then Stalin found out my grandfather was not in the Party. 'How can someone write a book like that and not be a communist?' he asked. Well, my grandfather joined the party rapidly.

My father was a painter and very anti-communist. He got no work whereas one of his friends was very successful in painting boring pictures of Lenin for institutions all over the Soviet Union. The joke was that he only used two colours, grey and red. But by the mid 1980s my father's friend could get no more work, while my father was losing much of his eyesight but still painting. Other artists would ask how he could still paint so well in such a condition. How could they, with their eyesight, not paint such pictures. My father would say he did not paint with his eyes. He did not see with his eyes. This is like me - I'll tell you later. I now have his paintings with me in my studio, and I have exhibited some of them here at my exhibition. I also have different books by my grandfather including the one I told you about. It was translated into many languages.

So tell me about the paintings at your exhibition?
Well, firstly there are the drawings and paintings of Petersburg. I really miss it so much. You can see a picture here of the bridge at Lomonosov. I used to live just near there. The picture I've done is watercolour at night. Here there's one of the canal or river Moika. This is a pen drawing. These are all memories for me.

Then there are the paintings of Bulgaria - the Rhodope mountains that we just talked about. I've tried to portray the woman of the mountains. You can see the shape of her body in many of the mountain views when you travel in the area around Smolian and there's one scene of her face, neck and breast, all in profile, which is incredible when you see it for yourself. It's symbolic. Body and landscape simultaneously. There are many places to find this harmony in the lines of the hills. In Bulgaria I get a feeling in the soul from the beauty of its natural life. I've also tried to capture the season changes. In my art I use the energy that radiates from the mountains, like in different seasons. Every day, every moment is different. Never the same, like life itself, always different light. Different times, different light. It's amazing to think that these browns and yellows in one of the paintings were all white a few hours later. So I've called the exhibition, *Through the window of the soul* because that's the effect some of this has on me. Seeing so much by feeling spiritually what happens inside me when I look at some of these scenes in life.

This is connected with the poems I wrote some time ago when I was in Russia. The constant theme of change and never staying the same, like clouds, always moving, never the same from from one moment to the next. It's like looking through windows, through the soul. Two of these three poems are here at the exhibition next to the paintings.

> In the bright window of your soul
> Like a light cloud, elusive,
> Smiling, I sail past.
>
> I will remember always, I promise,
> That it is like a dream
> That I cannot return to it.

The next one has the theme of the continuing changes in nature and people, but like an exchange between people, a harmony between different views. It refers to the two rivers in Petersburg, the Fontanka and the Neva and the white light you can get in Petersburg at night. This poem appeared in a Russian newspaper (*Smena*) in 1988 along with my picture of the Moika in Petersburg.

Fontanka behind us
Consumed in the Neva
My bank - great stone
Yours - dressed in foliage

River makes poetry with water
It writes loud waves
Differently we hear one melody

Not the same winter wind blows for us
And the sun warms us in different ways
For you it is light in the sunrise
For us in the sunset

But if day is finished
Both our banks will be submerged
In the white night
Like a river of milk

In mother of pearl waves
Rocked all around
Will give dreams for the morning
About the other side

There with movement
A small coloured light of the night
Swims across.

Finally, I think you might like this one. It's based on a story *Zobada* by Karlo Gocci. The story is of a man changing women into animals. One woman finds out and cannot decide whether to change or stay. I think this is so appropriate to what we've talked about and perhaps provides a fitting end to our thoughts about society, its dangers, and what to do about it, especially for me as a woman.

> I know 'man', insidious, sorcerer,
> For many women creating a thirst for revenge
> I don't know why, when or where he makes his sorcery for them.
>
> In the black grottos of his eyes and the dark of his soul
> How many of us got lost and died?
> You were beautiful but now let us hiss like a snake
> And let us, my dear, like goats, at last, butt back.
>
> My dear what is in your hand?
> I take the potion, and what shall I become?
> Let us stay at a distance
> As I think I will stay as a tigress.

The poems were translated by Liudmila Vasileva and Richard Minns

Five Poems

Foreign Correspondent

We are inventing for ourselves a story.
The other life. A narrative that frets and stumbles
yet moves along at such a pace, I'm winded.

Water keeps the distance words try to close.

A peace-keeping force means soldiers in,
then soldiers out. The arms embargo's off.
A meteor falls, another sign to read.

I do, I read and read, your words, the heavens'.

Remember, this is the oldest of games:
paper, scissors, stone,
the power of hands pretending.

Maura Dooley

Srebrenica Farewell

What is it on certain days that motivates the heart to regret?
Across the nation men and women awake to clarity,
to see the horrors they have committed. Each shame
is suffered alone.

Sometimes, in confidence, it is relieving
to admit atrocity, to claim sin. But not on these mornings
when the stomach drops and the ground feels as though it might decide
not to hold you up. Children never wake like this.

Men remember every screw they ever stole. It is a bright
sunny day when rapes in far away lands have a name:
Hava Usmanovic, Mina Smailovic and her sister Fata,
Mrs Masanovic, Edita Masanovic, Hanifa Gadzo, Mrs Hasj.

It is a day when you rush about cleaning your house because
all laziness is unforgiveable. No matter how fast you move
you cannot out-run your pulse.

Srebrenica, it appears that we will abandon you.
What area is safe when soldiers won't be sacrificed?
Since when were soldiers not meant to die in war?

There are not enough scarves for all the girls to hang themselves.

We have all woken to mornings like this. Some of us
go back to sleep until the day ends, again, half-curtained.

Tanya Stepan

Sutton's Seeds

Here her petunias melt -
petals soft as octopus webbing.
By mid-afternoon they droop
like eyelids with sleeping sickness.

She waters them in the shade
wearing a frayed straw brim
and pale amethysts.
They collapse and collapse,
flower-fountains spilling
from packets sent out by English friends.

At night she smooths moisturizing cream
into her forehead, neck and cheeks,
recalling the way her sweetpeas
used to sow themselves, pastels
tangling a chickenwire trellis;
the sundial oozing moss, shadowless.

As she unclasps the watery amethysts,
creases around her mouth
turn into expressions,
the accumulation of unspoken words.

On the balcony her petunias gasp;
even the stars prickle.

Gregory Warren Wilson

The Lace Maker

Purblind, he cannot cage, coop or kennel me.
Tone-deaf, he cannot overhear or eavesdrop

on my mind. I am only a mezzo tint to his
myopic gaze, moving round his house, altering

the paintings on the walls from time to time.
The lace maker has inhabited every room but one,

bent over her work for centuries now. Mesh, net
and knot are stilled under her hand. Unlined,

her brow bends as her hands move, her hair plaited
and parted and curled, mapped, charted and surveyed.

Ingenuous but competent in her candour, she forestalls
his anger, shackles and trammels her bright flawed eye.

Her ageless immaculacy, nonesuch, nonpareil, obscures
my uneven makeshift defence against his cudgels of wit.

I bind his eyes. I block his ears. I move around
making words like lace, small and similar and spurned.

Elizabeth Bartlett

The Robin

and when I let my Black Monk tempt to misery,
run from the perfection I have set for me,
and sit to weep my weak-kneed inability to cope,
the robin, on impossibly thin limbs, comes, trampolining.

Roy Blackman

When science fails us

Richard Levins

*Richard Levins looks at the dramatic failures of
Euro-North American science, and argues for a
science that looks more broadly at our relationship
with the rest of nature. This is an edited version of
his address on receiving the 1996 Edinburgh Medal.*

Modern Euro-North American science has developed technologies which seemed
to promise a deeper understanding of the world and a better life for humanity.
And indeed its achievements are impressive: we can read the composition of distant
galaxies from tired bits of ancient light, we can decipher the histories of the rocks
formed a billion years ago and the diets of species long gone. We can track the
movements of molecules and of caribou, sequences of genes and civilizations. We
have bred plants and animals to fit our technologies, invented new ways of
communicating and of diagnosing diseases and predicting the weather.

But science also has had dramatic failures. The promises of understanding and
progress have not been kept, and the application of science to human affairs has
often done great harm. Public health has been caught by surprise by the resurgence
of old diseases and the appearance of new ones; modern planning has not given us
more liveable cities; industrial design for greater efficiency has not made work more
humane but has instead led to increased bodily stress, anxiety, overwork and
unemployment; pesticides increase pests, create new pest problems and contribute
to the load of poison in our habitat; antibiotics create new pathogens resistant to
our drugs; modern high-tech agronomy watches our soils disappearing; the green
revolution did not eliminate hunger but increased the polarisation of rich and poor,

and the dependence of developing countries on imports; scientific theories have been put forth to justify inequality, racism, aggression and competitiveness.

I am sure that all of you could add to the list of major problems that science has not only not solved but has even made worse through the invention of technologies that intervene strongly into complex processes with simple-minded expectations. It is no wonder that we see an anti-science backlash, with cuts in expenditures for research and the education of scientists, the turning of young people away from the scientific vocations, a counterposing of scientific knowledge to humane or spiritual feelings and morality, and attacks on scientific rationality itself.

It is natural that scientists and other intellectuals rush to the defence of science, but some of the criticisms are valid. There are, broadly, two very different kinds of criticism, one conservative and one radical, from very different sources and pursuing very different goals. Conservative criticism rejects the very goal of science, to understand the world in order to guide our actions. Its advocates often brush aside scientific evidence in favour of theological claims. They misuse the mathematics of 'chaos' to deny the essential intelligibility of the world. They recognise the social conditioning and the ultimate fallibility of science, but use this as an excuse for refusing to distinguish the relatively true from the dreadfully wrong. These critics usually praise technology while damning the intellectual independence of science which made that technology possible. Their ideal would be technically well trained, docile and specialised researchers inventing ever newer and more sophisticated means while remaining unreflective about ends.

Radical criticism, however, shares the old scientific goals of understanding the world for making life better. It taxes science for its failure to live up to its own stated principles. It argues that military secrecy and corporate proprietary rights directly deny access to knowledge and that the high cost of research denies it in practice. This means that we can no longer undertake the independent verification that was the cornerstone of the democracy of science, and the guarantor of its objectivity. The costs of an education, and economic inequalities, make access to the scientific community a matter of privilege. Furthermore, hierarchies of credibility and rich vocabularies for putting down uncomfortable ideas - 'far out', 'faddish', 'cranky', 'not mainstream' , 'ideological' or 'unproven' - negate the spirit of open-minded inquiry, while the need for continued funding and prestige makes it important to be first and to be right rather than to be self-critical and open. Thus a cult of expertise and credentials thwarts the democratic, egalitarian spirit of science, so that arguments are not given equal opportunity regardless of their source.

This criticism also challenges some of the core principles of science themselves. For example, the demand to examine ideas without reference to their source, an expression of elementary fairness, also prevents us from understanding the context of innovation, the reasons for science following one agenda and not another. The call to separate thinking from feeling or facts from wishes, so crucial in the struggle for objectivity, encourages the passive impersonal mode of scientific writing that hides the history of and reasons for an investigation. It has allowed scientists to participate in the most heinous crimes with a sense of righteousness.

A good radical criticism aims at a democratic, humane and creative science that looks at our relation with the rest of nature in its broadest context, that would combine specialised research with self-reflection and with frequent re-examination of goals. It seeks a renovation of science that revives some of the old traditional goals but also proposes new ones.

In what follows I will discuss three areas where scientific disciplines have had great success in the small but failed us in the large; I will then consider some of the common features in their failure, and, finally, suggest a programme for the revitalisation of science.

The epidemiological transition

Two or three decades ago the expectation was that infectious disease would decline and be replaced by chronic disease as the major health problem in the world. This expectation was labelled the epidemiological transition and remained the prevailing dogma in public health even after the resurgence of malaria, tuberculosis, cholera and dengue, and the appearance of AIDS, Lyme disease, Ebola virus, Marburg virus, Lassa fever, toxic shock syndrome and Legionnaire's disease. As each new disease appeared it was studied urgently and knowledge of the infective agent, its means of transmission and approaches to treatment appeared quickly. Genes were sequenced, tests invented and surveillance systems designed to detect new cases rapidly. But new diseases continue to appear and old ones reinvade.

That science was caught by surprise by the resurgence of infectious disease is in itself not surprising. Surprise in science is inevitable because we have to study the new by treating it just like the old. This makes science necessary and simple experience insufficient. But it also makes surprise inevitable and guarantees that we eventually meet situations where our old ideas no longer hold and perhaps never did.

However we do have the obligation to understand why enormous errors were made, and to recognise and correct them as soon as possible. In order to do this, we first have to understand why the idea that infection would decline seemed so plausible in the 1970s. My working hypothesis is that our scientific predecessors were just as smart as we are, and if they reached the wrong conclusions, they did so for good reasons. There were three supporting arguments. Firstly, it could be seen that infectious disease had been declining for over a century. Smallpox was on the verge of complete eradication, tuberculosis was in retreat, a polio vaccine removed the annual panic of infantile paralysis. Secondly, new drugs, antibiotics, better vaccines, more subtle diagnostic techniques were being invented to increase our tool kit, while our adversaries, the bacteria and viruses and fungi, had to rely on the same old tools of mutation and recombination - surely this would tip the balance in our favour. Thirdly, it was proclaimed that international economic development programmes would end poverty, and the new affluence would allow all countries the resources to apply the most modern techniques of disease control. It would also give us longer lives and an older population. Since most infectious diseases attack children, we would be less vulnerable to them.

These were plausible arguments, but they were wrong. And the ways in which they were wrong prove very enlightening.

A century or two is too short a time period to justify the claim of a definitive end to infectious disease. If we look instead at the longer sweep of human history we see diseases rise and fall. The first pandemic of plague that we can confirm in Europe emerged and subsided during the collapse of the Roman empire, the second as feudalism entered its crisis in the fourteenth century. The conquest of the Americas was perhaps the most devastating epidemiological event of recorded history. Plague, smallpox, tuberculosis and other diseases combined with the hunger caused by the breakup of indigenous productive systems, and direct massacres, to reduce the population by as much as 90 per cent in the two centuries following Columbus. This public health disaster lasted two centuries and in some ways is not completely over.

Thus the doctrine of the epidemiological transition is better replaced by the proposition that whenever there are large-scale changes in society, climate, land use or population movements there will also be new epidemiological problems.

It was not the lack of knowledge of history that caused this lack of attention to the long sweep of history. There was a sense that our own time represented so radical a break with the past that what happened back then was irrelevant, or, in the words of Henry Ford, 'history is bunk!'

There were other aspects to the narrowness of thinking about disease. Medical science is concerned only with one species, the human. But if public health workers had looked also at veterinary and plant disease, it would have been more obvious that disease is a general phenomenon of evolutionary ecology. All groups of animals and plants have parasites. There are even bacteria that parasitize protozoa, others that infect roundworms, and bacteria and viruses that parasitize bacteria. Parasitism involves complex patterns of adaptation and counter-adaptation, with no evidence for a long-term trend to their elimination. Looking at

'A century or two is too short a time period to justify the claim of a definitive end to infectious disease'

a wider range of species, health workers would have seen diseases spreading and contracting, spilling over into new hosts and presenting different symptoms and microbes competing with or enhancing each other's capacity for mischief. They would have been sensitive to the epidemiological consequences of deforestation, irrigation, new patterns of human settlement. The experience of agriculture, that pests become resistant to pesticides, would have reinforced the observations of drug and antibiotic resistance to warn that whenever we change the conditions of survival for an organism, the evolutionary pressures on it will be changed and it will respond one way or another.

Disease is not merely a question of a pathogen finding a host; nor is medicine a question of a drug killing the pathogen. Whether a germ successfully establishes itself in a person, and whether it is able to invade a population, depends on the vulnerabilities of both. This is influenced by the status of the individual's immune system, which may be depressed by other diseases, malnutrition, stress, drugs and pollutants, and by other less well studied aspects of disease resistance.

Another aspect of the narrowness of thinking about disease is the separation of the biological from the social. A social epidemiology would begin with the proposition that human biology is a socialised biology. This is true of our physiology: eating is not understandable merely as the biochemistry of nutrition. What we eat or refuse to eat, who eats and who does not eat, how much we eat, who determines what is eaten, who you eat with or wouldn't be caught dead eating with, who prepares the food and who washes up, are all consequences not only of the physiological fact that we have to eat, but also of the social arrangements around eating. Breathing is not a passive result of respiratory metabolism. How we breathe is related to stress, air quality, perceptions about the social environment and our emotions. Posture and biomechanical stress, the back aches and stiff necks and painful joints and muscles, are not the passive consequence of our species walking erect but of who we are in society, what kind of work we do and what feelings we are expressing or suppressing, and what we are trying to convey with our postures. Pantomime actors grasp this exquisitely, and in an instant convey to their audiences whether they own an estate or are slaves on that estate, whether they are important, dangerous, accommodating or insignificant. More obviously, sex cannot be understood simply as reproduction.

Human genetics and ecology are also social. If epidemiologists had been more sensitive to how society penetrates our bodies, genes would not have been so readily accepted as independent and sufficient explanations of patterns of prevalence of diseases. All genes do is make proteins or influence when the proteins are made. What happens next depends on the environments within the cell, in the body as a whole, and in the community where that body develops and on the complex interactions among genes, the organism as a whole and the environment. Genes may influence which environments an organism is exposed to. These environments then affect the rate of mutation of the genes. They determine which genetic differences show up as organism differences, and which genes are selected.

We have transformed our environments. The composition of our outdoor and indoor atmosphere has been supplemented by tens of thousands of new chemical compounds which interact in unsuspected ways. Productive activity takes place at temperatures, at paces, and at hours of the day and night that are historically new for our thermoregulatory mechanisms, our serotonin rhythms and our muscles. Giant cities and the special habitats of prisons, nursing homes, schools and refugee camps offer previously unexperienced population densities. Sealed buildings and barely recycled air in aeroplanes create new habitats for pathogens and increase exposures to airborne viruses. New patterns of alienation, social harassment and anxiety demand that our physiological and psychological responses that evolved for emergencies cope with chronic conditions. If we could step back from the details and squint we would see patterns: our societies make us sicker in a thousand ways and then invest ever more resources trying to repair the damage.

A social epidemiology could be sensitive to the complexity of the pathways linking general aspects of society through our nervous systems and neurotransmitters to the various kinds of white blood cells that fight infection and sometimes turn against us. The outcomes of infection depend on these same factors and also on the availability and effectiveness of medical care. And they obviously are not distributed evenly across countries or within countries. They are certainly not distributed evenly across diseases, where the pattern of knowledge and ignorance is influenced by whose diseases they are.

The expectation that the new technologies of drugs, antibiotics, pesticides and vaccines would 'win the war' with the pathogens grossly underestimated the dynamic capacity of organisms to adapt and the intricacies of natural selection. Microbes not only undergo mutation but also can receive genes from other species. Therefore genetic variation is available for selection. Therapies that threaten the survival of the germs also focus natural selection on overcoming or evading those therapies. The genetic make-up of pathogen populations therefore shifts readily, not only in the long run but even in the course of a single outbreak and within a single host during a bout of illness. Strong opposing demands on the pathogen's biology select for access to nutrients, avoidance of the body's defences and exit to a new host. Variations in the state of nutrition, the immune system, the presence or absence of other infections, access to treatment, the treatment regime and conditions of transmission push and pull the genetic make-up of pathogen populations in different directions so that we constantly see new strains arising that differ in their drug and antibiotic resistance, clinical course, virulence, and biochemical detail. Some even develop resistance to treatments that have not yet been used if these threaten the survival of the pathogens in ways similar to old treatments. As long as we see nature as passively absorbing the impacts of our interventions we will be caught by surprise by the failures of previously successful interventions.

The third reason that public health professionals expected the decline of infectious disease was the belief that the economic penetration of capitalism to the furthest reaches of the globe would eliminate hunger and provide health care for all people in all classes in all countries. This assertion was accepted implicitly without examination. It was part of the cold war mythology, and therefore challenges to it could be dismissed as enemy propaganda. Only now can mainstream social science acknowledge the growing gap between rich and poor countries, and within countries, and ask why the earlier expectations have not been realised. And only now can public health confront the growing inequalities as a serious public health issue.

Thus public health was caught by surprise because of several kinds of narrowness: a short time frame, limitation to only our own species, isolation from evolutionary ecology, and a failure to come to grips with the pressing social issues that affect vulnerability. In order to be up to the task it faces, an integrated epidemiology would have long time horizons, broad species ranges, be rooted in evolutionary ecology and social theory, respect and study explicitly the structure and dynamics of complex systems, and look critically at its own history. These are characteristics of what would be a dialectical epidemiology.

Of green revolutions

The problems and failures that beset public health have much in common with those in agriculture because agriculture is like medicine in many ways. The objects of interest in both fields are simultaneously biological and social. Both agriculture and health researchers are trying to solve urgent problems of human welfare and therefore are often impatient of theory. Both have received generous public support as well as private corporate investment. The products of that massive research effort mostly have been turned into commodities and marketed for private gain.

In both medicine and agriculture practice often does more harm than good, often enough that we have special terms to describe these failures: iatrogenesis, the causing of disease by doctors; nosocomial infections that arise in hospitals; secondary pests that become threats to food production only after intensive pesticide use. In both fields, we have achieved great sophistication in the small, but this has been accompanied by a growing irrationality in the large. Finally, dissatisfaction with both fields has led to the growth of 'alternative' movements such as herbal medicine, homeopathy, naturopathy, organic and biodynamic farming.

Over the last few centuries average agricultural yields increased as a result of the application of mechanisation, chemicalisation (fertilisers and pesticides), plant and animal breeding, and scientific management. Although problems arose, it was widely believed that these were the costs of progress and would be solved by the same means that created them. But starting in the 1960s there has been increasing criticism of the high-tech pathway of agricultural development. The different criticisms have come from different sources with different concerns, but also flow together into a coherent theoretical and political critique:

1. Modern high-tech agriculture has not eliminated hunger.
2. It undermines its own productive base through erosion, soil compaction and salinisation, depletion of water resources and of genotypic diversity.
3. It changes land use patterns, encouraging deforestation, draining of wetlands, planting crops according to market criteria even in unsuitable climates. It promotes a loss of crop diversity by specialisation and commercial seed production and reduces overall biodiversity through its chemical inputs and extensive monocultures.
4. It increases vulnerability to nature, especially to climate and microclimate change, pest outbreaks and atmospheric and water pollutants because of large scale monoculture, the selection of varieties for maximum yield under optimal conditions and the loss of beneficial fauna and flora.
5. It makes farming increasingly dependent on off-the-farm inputs, and therefore on cash flow, as fertilisers replace natural nitrogen fixers, irrigation replaces the broken hydrological flows and storages of water, pesticides replace natural enemies of pests and hybrid seeds must be bought. Dependence on external inputs increases the vulnerability to price instability and politically motivated trade policies.
6. It debases food quality as regional specialisation increases storage and transport time, crops and techniques are chosen for quantitative yield, and specialisation makes even farmers dependent on food purchases.
7. It increases the gap between rich and poor. The rich are able to buy or get credit to buy the new inputs, establish the marketing connections and average their returns across years while the poor need to be successful every year. It especially undermines the economic independence of women. The new technologies are usually given to men even where women traditionally did most of the farming. The new technologies make the domestic chores of women, such as gathering firewood and fetching water, more time consuming; and women's diverse activities in the home conflict with the extreme seasonality of commercial monoculture.

8. It poisons people, first the farm workers who handle pesticides, then their family members who handle the pesticide soaked clothing and drink water where pesticides and fertilisers have run into ground water. Finally it reaches those who eat the crops produced with pesticides and animals raised with antibiotics and growth hormones.

9. It poisons other species and the environment as a whole, with eutrophication of our waterways from fertiliser runoff, accumulation of pesticides in the body tissues of fish and birds, and nitrification of the air.

Despite its technical complexity, modern agricultural technology has a narrow intellectual base susceptible to surprise. The final conclusion is that the commercialised, export-oriented high-tech agriculture is a non-sustainable successional stage in the ecology of production, like the shrubs that squeeze out the grasses and herbs of an abandoned field only to create the conditions for their own replacement by trees.

What I have described as a successional stage is seen by proponents of modernisation as a desirable end goal. Modernisation theory assumes that there is only a single pathway of development, along the single axis from less developed to more developed, and that the task of the less developed is to become like the more developed as quickly as possible. Modernisation theory proposes that:

1. Progress moves from labour-intensive to capital-intensive production.

2. Progress moves from heterogeneous land use to homogeneous land use devoted to the most advantageous crop.

3. Progress moves from small scale to large scale to take advantage of the economies of scale.

4. Progress moves from dependence on nature to control over or replacement of nature.

5. Progress requires the replacement of traditional knowledge, labelled 'superstition', by scientific knowledge.

6. In science, modernisation theory asserts that progress moves from broad general knowledge to increasingly narrow specialisation, and

7. Progress moves from the study of natural objects to their smallest parts.

But an integrated, agricultural science equally rooted in natural science and a critique of society would recognise that we have to move beyond the capital-intensive model where great masses of energy are applied to move great quantities of matter, to a low input, gentle, thought-intensive technology that nudges more than it commands and reduces dependence on purchased equipment and chemicals. Such a system is less energy-costly, preserves productive capacity, and protects the human population and our habitats.

An integrated agricultural science would reject both the random heterogeneity of land use imposed by land tenure, and the homogeneity of the plantation. It would propose a planned heterogeneity in a mosaic of land uses where each plot of land contributes harvestable products and also facilitates the production on the other plots. Forests would provide wood and fruit and honey but also modulate the flow of water, alter the microclimate out from the edge, house birds and bats that consume pests, and offer restful shelter to people. Pastures could provide livestock, manure for biogas and to fertilise vegetable beds, nectar sources for parasitic wasps that control pests, fix nitrogen and control erosion. Elements of such a system are already in practice in many places. In Cuba, alternating strips of bananas and sweet potatoes or intercrops of corn with sweet potatoes provide the shade and nesting sites that allow predatory ants to control pests of sweet potato. Occasional rows of corn among the peppers divert the fruitworms from the peppers. Organic farmers in the United States use marigolds to repel nematodes and beans to protect tomatoes from the late blight as well as to fix nitrogen. Maize roots reach deep down and bring up minerals from lower layers while shallow rooted crops hold the soil. Ponds produce fish and predatory dragonflies, ameliorate the microclimate, are a reservoir of water for fire fighting and a place to swim.

The unit of planning need not coincide with the unit of production. The sizes of plots need to reflect the scales over which beneficial interactions occur. The mosaic of different land uses can combine considerations of crop rotation, buffers against natural and economic uncertainty, a diverse diet, differential labour requirements, and compensating diversity of more and less profitable crops.

Modernisation's attempt to remove our subjection to the uncertainties of nature by a complete control over all the processes on a farm cannot be successful. But we can confront uncertainty through a mixed strategy, of detection of problems in time to do something about them, prediction of likely events, design of a buffered system tolerant to a broad range of conditions, and by prevention. All of this requires intellectual detours from the narrowly practical to understand the long and short term processes in their rich complexity. This is part of what I mean by a dialectical perspective.

An integrated agro-ecology would respect both traditional and scientific knowledge. The one is derived from a detailed, intimate, perceptive and very specific familiarity that people have with their own circumstances; while the other requires some distance from the particular in order to compare and generalise. Each has its areas of insight and its blindnesses, so that the best conditions for producing knowledge are those that allow farmers and scientists to meet as equals.

Agriculture has to be guided by a broader scientific vision. We must reject the reductionism that gives priority to molecules over cells and cells over organisms and organisms over populations. I insist that in addition to modern molecular biology there is also a modern physiology, modern anatomy, modern ecology, modern biogeography, modern sociology.

Protecting the environment

Environmental awareness is not new. Movements for the preservation of nature, usually of the relatively unexploited parts of nature, have existed for over a century. Concern for the inhabited environment also has a long history. In the US the Environment Protection Agency was established in 1970, and there are now many international agencies concerned with one or another aspect of environmental protection. The Soviet Union had some of the earliest and most stringent and thoughtful (and unenforced) laws for environmental protection since the 1920s. Costa Rica has adopted a bold programme to set aside vast areas as national parks. Nevertheless, industry continues to pour CO_2 into the atmosphere, the forests still blacken under acid rain or yield to the chainsaw, fish populations decline and carcinogens accumulate, and Costa Rica is leading the world in the rate of loss of rain forest to banana plantations and impoverished peasants.

There also have been dramatic reversals of the destructive trends. There are salmon in the Thames again, and reforestation in Japan. The Hudson River is cleaner and smog has declined in London. It seems as if no local environmental problem - except for some of the radioactive contamination sites - is completely unremediable. However, each time a forest or pond is saved it becomes harder to save the next one. Arguments are offered about 'going too far', or play off the environment against 'the economy'. Corporations that have never cared a fig about their workers suddenly become champions of job protection in order to have a free hand to cut down forests.

The history of environmental degradation is a history of greed, poverty and ignorance. By greed I do not mean the individual idiosyncratic greed that might yearn for three yachts where two would do. Rather I refer to the institutionalised greed of business that has to expand to survive, that is always looking for new products, ways to

'Each time a forest or pond is saved it becomes harder to save the next one'

create new needs, ways to cut costs by reducing environmental safeguards or evading the enforcement of existing ones. At a time when there is growing awareness of the need for an 'ecological society', the incompatibility of that goal with an economy driven by greed has not yet been assimilated. Proposals are still being offered to reconcile two very different modes of relating to nature.

While ecological necessity seeks sustainability, the commodified economy needs growth. This growth can be achieved by producing more of the same things, by making familiar commodities bigger, more complicated or with more elaborate packaging. Growth can be achieved by inventing new ways of turning natural conditions into resources for exploitation, by finding technical means for making more and more of our lives marketable, and by investing great effort into creating new needs for consumption.

While ecology stresses interaction, environmental protection law depends on assessing separable liabilities. The courts cannot disentangle the complexities of nature, so that sometimes awareness of interaction protects the polluters more than the environment.

While ecology values the uniqueness of materials, places and living things, the economy sees them all as interchangeable commodities measured on the single scale of economic values. Therefore there is no special virtue in preserving a resource. It may be economically rational to use up a resource totally and then move to the next investment.

While ecology values diversity, economic rationality favours going for the single most profitable crop, and great quantities of a single commodity, to benefit from economies of scale.

There exist movements resisting untrammelled greed. The destruction of particular habitats has been halted, some noxious substances have been removed from the atmosphere, important victories have been won. But growth itself cannot be retarded, the valuing of nature on the single scale of money cannot be eliminated, and new hazards can be invented faster than they can be studied and outlawed. Thus the complexities and anomalies of protecting our environment arise from a deep conflict between the ecology and the economy.

The ignorance which contributes to environmental degradation is not the passive absence of information but a constructed mix of data, gaps in data, data about irrelevant things, unrealistic expectations, fragmented knowledge, rigid categories and false dichotomies. It hides the impacts of economic activities and technical choices and narrows the scope of inquiry. It also obscures the processes of choosing among alternatives by the use of euphemisms such as 'the economy' to stand for profit, 'decision makers' for the owners or their representatives. It hides within the language of cost/benefit analysis the separation between those who pay the costs and those who get the benefits and pretends that a neutral optimisation process reconciles the interests of all parties when more usually all it can do is ratify existing relations of power.

The general critique

The problems of health, agriculture and environment are complex problems. But so is engineering. Before the space ship Challenger exploded it was quite common to hear the exasperated query, 'But how come we can put a man on the moon and yet not...' The 'yet not' could be to eliminate hunger or cure AIDS or save the rainforest or any other of a growing list of stubborn problems. The question was usually rhetorical, not a search for an answer but a cry of protest against misplaced priorities. But it is a serious question and deserves careful attention. I think there are three major reasons for the intractability of these problems.

First, there is the acceptance of hidden and unacknowledged side conditions. We want to provide health care for all, but subject to the side condition that the pharmaceutical industry continues private and profitable, and in backward countries such as mine that health insurance and even medical service itself are provided for gain. We want to preserve rural life, subject to not infringing on the power of the landed oligarchies. We want to respect the cultures and land rights of indigenous peoples, subject to the side conditions that the oil monopolies can use the subsoil unimpeded. We want to encourage food production, subject to the side conditions that imported food products can enter the third world markets freely and compete with peasant cultivators. We want a poison-free atmosphere, provided we do not intrude on the trade secrets of the polluters.

The second set of reasons is institutional. Ministries of health do not usually speak to ministries of agriculture and doctors do not talk to veterinarians or plant pathologists. This is especially a problem in the United States where plant pathology and veterinary medicine are taught in the universities of the land grant system run by state governments while medical schools are mostly in private urban universities. Corporations guard their product information from each other and the public. The systems of rewards and promotions for scientists place a premium on short term reductionist research that is most readily turned into marketable commodities. The tables of organisation of a research centre or university reflect and reinforce barriers among disciplines. Further, the studies of different objects are often arrayed on a hierarchical scale with ranking by the size of the object (the smaller ones being more 'fundamental') or along a 'hardness-softness' axis. In biology, the students of the small have appropriated the term 'modern' for their own fields.

Finally we come to the intellectual barriers to solving these problems. The problems are complex in ways different from those in engineering where the parts are produced outside of the wholes and perform in the laboratory more or less the way they will perform in the assembled systems. In eco-social systems it is not always clear what the appropriate 'parts' are, since they evolve and develop together and have only temporary existence away from their 'wholes'. The objects that have to be analysed together, such as the microbes themselves, the nutritional levels of populations and the behaviour of health bureaucrats, have been assigned to different disciplines.

The barriers all derive from the very powerful reductionist strategy that created Euro-North American science in the first place and made possible its dramatic successes but also its special blindnesses. The choice of the smallest possible object as the 'problem', the division of a problem into its smallest parts for analysis, the holding constant of everything but one factor at a time, the examination of static descriptions before the looking at the dynamics, the subdivision of the research process itself into the separate stages of assembling the 'facts' and the making of theories, all had their historical justifications in the struggle for scientific objectivity against several adversaries, including theological authoritarianism and also the introspections of natural philosophy and other unanchored speculations. The reductionist tactics have temporary value as moments in the scientific process. There is nothing wrong with identifying cell types or sequencing DNA or measuring energy. They are research tactics, and may be useful or not according to the specific situation. But as a philosophy of nature and society, and as the dominant mode of investigation, they are responsible for many of the dramatic failures of scientific programmes.

> 'things are the way they are because they got this way, not because they always were or have to be or will always be this way'

It is necessary in all research to make distinctions, to identify objects of interest as separate from other objects, to recognise different kinds of processes and causes. But science often stops there, without then putting back together what it has separated physically or conceptually. It imagines that our own creations, what we do for purposes of study, are valid descriptions of reality. False dichotomies such as heredity/environment, physical/psychological, equilibrium/change, science/ideology, thinking/feeling, biological/social, random/determined, order/chaos, lawfulness/historical contingency, life style/social conditions, have wrought havoc with scientific analysis, forcing choices between alternatives that really are not mutually exclusive. Instead of confronting the richness of interaction and interpenetration, scientific analysis often resorts to statistical devices to assign relative weights to different factors. Once we have done this, we can imagine that we have described complexity when what we have really done is reduce that complexity to a sum of 'factors'. Criticism of these and other false dichotomies is both a necessary step in the revitalisation of science to make it capable of confronting the enormous problems our species is now facing, and a major aspect of a dialectical approach.

But when we abandon the reductionist programme we are confronted with phenomena of daunting complexity, and without the tools for examining that complexity. The study of complexity requires a focus on change. We have to ask two fundamental questions about the world: why are things the way they are instead of a little bit different, and why are things the way they are instead of very different. The first is the question of self-regulation, of homeostasis, of the network of positive and negative feedbacks that absorb, transform, relocate and negate perturbations so that systems remain recognisably what they are despite the constant buffeting of opposing forces. It is the domain of systems theory proper, which takes a system as given and asks how it behaves. The second is the question of evolution, history, development, non-equilibrium theory. It starts from the simple proposition that things are the way they are because they got this way, not because they always were or have to be or will always be this way. The 'things' are both the objects of study and ourselves, the scientists who study them. The two questions are of course not independent. The long-term processes create the variables of the persistent systems. The processes that keep aspects of systems intact also change other aspects and eventually change the identities and connections among the parts. The self-regulating processes not only preserve the equilibria but also the directions of change of equilibria. Equilibrium is a form of motion, a relatively stable relation among changing things.

Revitalising science

At present science is being pulled in opposite directions. On the one hand, economic pressures are undermining the traditional - always exaggerated but none the less real - relative autonomy of scientists. The single-minded concern of governments to cut costs and to privatise is shifting control of science as a whole, and the conditions of work of scientists, to administrators who see science as an industry like any other industry and scientists as a scientific workforce to be managed like any other workforce. The product of the science industry is knowledge that can become commodities mostly as physical objects but also as services and reports. The economic rationality of the administration encourages the fragmentation of scientific workshops, specialisation, short-term precisely defined goals, decisions based less on intellectual or social necessity and more on marketability and risk avoidance. They manage scientific labour with the familiar devices they use in any industry - a myopic view of 'efficiency', downsizing, use of part time and temporary researchers and teachers, hierarchical rankings that keep the producers divided. Scientists learn quickly to plan research efforts based on criteria of acceptability and fundability, to rush publication to meet the timetables of appointments and promotions, to weigh carefully the costs and benefits of sharing and secrecy.

These trends are in conflict both with the internal intellectual needs of science for a more integrated, dynamic, dialectical outlook, and with the urgency to confront problems too big to face in a fragmented way. A science that is up to the mark would differ from the traditional Euro-North American science in a number of ways:

1. It would be frankly partisan. I propose the hypothesis that all theories are wrong which promote, justify or tolerate injustice. The wrongness may be in the data, its interpretation or its application, but if we search for that wrongness we will also be led to truth.

2. It would be democratic in at least three ways. First, access to the scientific community would be open to everyone with the scientific vocation without the barriers of class, racism or misogyny. Second, the results of science would be available to the whole population in a form that is intelligible and without the secrecy often justified in the name of national security or proprietary rights. Third, it would recognise that science prospers when it can combine the knowledge and insights of institutional science with those of the farmers, patients, and inhabitants of workplaces and communities that make up the 'alternative' movements. This is not quite the same thing as combining professional and nonprofessional understanding, since alternative movements have always been invigorated by professionals who ally with them. The result is a mobilisation of much more of the world's intelligence, creativity, and insight than ever before.

3. It must be polycentric. The centres of world science have shifted historically from the ancient middle east, south and east Asia and Central America to Germany, France, England and now Euro-North America. This monopoly of knowledge has served monopolies of power. It has often resulted in the imposition of foreign agendas on the scientific communities of the third world and has deprived us all of insights that are often less rigid, less fragmented and more dynamic and that arose in societies quite different from our own. Polycentric science must not become a sentimental orientalism or nationalism or deference to the ancient because it is ancient. Rather it must recognise that each social context produces its own pattern of insight and blindness, its own urgencies and indifferences, its own penetrating revelations and built-in confusions. A new global science must share techniques, knowledge and tools, be able to compare and choose, but also respectfully leave room for radically different approaches for facing the unknown.

4. It must be dialectical. The term dialectical materialism has had a bad reputation because of the way it was debased by Stalin and his school. The best dialecticians were eliminated or silenced, perhaps not singled out but caught up among others in a democracy of terror. It was then possible to reduce that rich perspective into a set of rigid rules and apologetics for decisions already taken on other grounds. However, as the most comprehensive self-conscious alternative to the predominant reductionism of cartesian science it has been the starting point for my own research. It offers the necessary emphasis on complexity, context, historicity, the interpenetration of seemingly mutually exclusive categories, the relative autonomy and mutual determination of different 'levels' of existence, and the contradictory, self-negating aspects of change.

5. It must be self-reflexive, recognising that the intervenors are part of the system and that the way we approach the rest of nature must also be accounted for. Thus it has to be doubly historical, looking at the history of the objects of interest and of our understanding of those objects.

This is a programme that runs counter to the prevailing trends in science, education and technology. Therefore it is not only an intellectual challenge but is also a highly political one which requires us to resist the pressures of the new world order. When the world recovers from the confusion that has accompanied the euphoric globalisation of greed, when the certainties of the present moment are once again in doubt, and our species joins together to continue its long quest for justice, equality, solidarity and now also survival, it is just possible that science will be there too, creating, receiving and sharing the knowledge that liberates.

The Edinburgh Medal is awarded by the City of Edinburgh Council to honour men and women of science who have made a significant contribution to the understanding and well-being of humanity. It was awarded in 1996 to Richard Levins, for his work on the integration of diverse sciences to create holistic models of population biology and ecosystems, in practical co-operation with farmers, and his lifelong commitment to science for the people. The Edinburgh Medal is one of the key events of the Edinburgh International Science Festival which takes place each year around Easter for two and a half weeks.

The Institute of International Visual Arts is an independent contemporary visual arts organisation which promotes the work of artists, academics and curators from a plurality of cultures and cultural perspectives. The Institute has four areas of activity: **exhibitions, publications, research and education and training** enabling it to work collaboratively with a range of institutions such as **galleries, publishers and universities, as well as individual artists, writers and curators.**

For further information on the Institute or to receive a copy of the *agenda* programme leaflet and our publications list, please contact us.

in**IVA**

Institute of International Visual Arts
Kirkman House, 12/14 Whitfield Stre
London W1P 5RD, United Kingdom
+44 171 636 1930 Voice
1931 Fax
email
institute@iniva.org

The Public Good

INTRODUCTION

Maureen Mackintosh

Welfare systems in divided societies necessarily embody complicated social settlements. In establishing the British National Health Service, Aneurin Bevan, with typical eloquence, summed this up. He called the book he wrote about the NHS *In Place of Fear*, a phrase evoking the health service's redistributive and insurance effects. And looking back on how he had managed to get the medical consultants on board, he famously remarked, 'I stuffed their mouths with gold'.[1] Public services contain within themselves the class divisions of their societies; but they *also* provide a space where those divisions are fought over, reduced and reworked. Effective public services bring together mutual insurance, redistribution and essential social investment (in skills, housing, public health, transport) in ways which string some links of solidarity across the social divides.

So when you unpick a welfare system you unpick a social settlement. That is what we have been doing in Britain, especially in the last fifteen years. Reforms of public services and benefits have reduced the security offered by the welfare state at a time of rising inequality and poverty, and high unemployment. The creation of self-governing schools and hospitals, and the introduction of market mechanisms into the big public services, have opened up some new spaces for innovation - but they have also increased management and administration relative to caring and teaching, and have generated widespread cynicism and declining standards.

Worst of all perhaps, we seem to have lost confidence in our ability to construct a public sphere which promotes the public good. For years now, the view that thoughtful public action could be valuable has been widely derided as naive. But no society can function without a public domain. In divided societies, not only public services, but public speech and action, voluntary association, and the regulation of the private sector are at the same time expressions of the economic and social divisions, and arenas for efforts to overcome them. In

---

1.   A. Bevan, *In Place of Fear*, Heinemann 1952; N. Timmins, *The Five Giants: A Biography of the Welfare State*, Fontana Press 1995, p115.

Britain, people have continued to pursue these efforts, but against a tide of malevolent divisiveness which has its roots in public policy.

This *Soundings* 'theme' section, called *The Public Good*, has two main objectives.[2] We set out to explore where we are going - in what ways are old settlements being unpicked, what new spaces have opened up, what is the bad and good in what is happening, how do we understand what futures are emerging? And second, what can be done? What are the crucial issues as we try to reconstruct a public domain: different from the old, less destructive than the present, not perfect, just better? We have tried not to rehearse current lines of debate, but instead to offer less familiar perspectives, to get off the tramlines.

Several themes emerge strongly from very diverse contributions. First, if we are to find a new 'social settlement' we can live with, we have to think clearly about social division. Britain is an acutely class-divided society, and layered into that are other profound divisions. To illustrate how public activity is infested with and reinforces these divisions - but still offers spaces for fighting back - the issue starts with one of the deepest divisions and one of the least explored in public policy: racism. In his recent and compelling biography of the British welfare state Nicholas Timmins notes that one could read his book and yet scarcely know 'that Commonwealth immigration, which greatly affected the welfare state and was greatly affected by it, took place.'[3] Gail Lewis explores just this issue, arguing that the social settlement represented by the British welfare state contains deeply embedded but shifting notions of 'race', which qualify welfare's apparent universalism, and which have been confronted by black activism. Francie Lund follows this with an activist's personal account of the struggle to overcome the vicious legacy of institutional racism within the South African public services.

Gail Lewis also introduces a second key theme of the issue: the need for new social settlements to accept and sustain difference and diversity. She argues for an explicit imagining of a welfare state that is both anti-racist, and resistant to racialising practices which categorise and contain people. The articles in the issue draw in very diverse voices, and this presence of difference is

---

2. I owe the shape and content of this issue to discussion with many friends and colleagues. Particular thanks to Pam Smith, Gail Lewis, Anne Showstack Sassoon and John Clarke who are however responsible only for their own contributions, and to Doreen Massey for enthusiasm, advice and support.
3. Timmins, *op. cit.*, p7.

reinforced by the extensive use of interviews and first person voices. One of the most resonant criticisms of the 'old' welfare state was its tendency to homogenisation and control; one of the good features amid the gloom of the last fifteen years has been more courage about diversity, innovation and risk. New social settlements have to build on that.

A very important source of innovation in welfare systems world-wide is the 'third sector': that mixture of charitable and voluntary activity, mutual associations, co-operative businesses, and self-governing non-profit trusts. Hard to define and much less well researched than the public and private sectors, the oddly named 'voluntary sector' offers space for social enterprise. This is the third key theme in the issue. Anne Showstack Sassoon argues that this messy patchwork stitches welfare systems together and creates essential links between big bureaucracies and individual needs. It also generates innovative forms and pressures which react back on and transform bureaucracies. Voluntary sector activists and researchers like Ann Hudock and Sarabajaya Kumar emphasise the way in which the 'market' reforms have opened up space for dialogue and new working relationships.

Lest we think there is something special about Britain, Carlo Borzaga shows that certain patterns of innovation are strikingly similar Europe-wide. The decline in welfare provision in the face of rising need has forced service users and providers into new relationships. He traces the widespread development of 'stakeholder co-operatives', bringing together users, workers, benefactors and sometimes public officials for the private non-commercial provision of welfare services.

This brings us to the fourth key theme of the issue: diversity within the *private* sector, and the deep intertwining of public, private and voluntary activity. In Britain - more than in other European countries - there is a tendency to see the 'public' and the 'private' as two separate boxes, hence to see private failures as having few public implications and *vice versa*. Several contributors emphatically disagree. Private sectors differ immensely between countries, and there are many ways in which British private business particularly fails to contribute to the public good: poor investment performance, short time horizons, inadequate training, poor external competitiveness, high unemployment. Privatising welfare has created new private abuses, such as unsuitable personal pensions.

We need mutually reinforcing reforms of private and public sectors. This point is central to all the contributions on pensions reform. Will Hutton argues that the British private sector needs longer-term investment horizons, which demands in turn a more 'insider' culture in private industry, where banks and pension fund trustees exercise more leverage over firms. But the private sector also needs democratising, with more accessible information, and better corporate governance. The snag is, can we *have* 'accountable insiders' in a culture where 'insider' tends to mean membership of a rather closed and self-serving elite? Several contributors describe their experience of trying to bring democracy, ethics and accountability into the private investment world.

H utton's question brings us back to *public* sector reform proper. He believes strongly that active reform of our public sphere, to break up privilege and democratise public action, is essential to make possible private sector institutional change. The fifth theme of this issue is that we have to have the courage to tackle some big reforms of the public services, if we are to stop the rot and reconstruct social solidarity in new forms. The health services articles chart some of the rot - and the despair which can block real change. The NHS reforms, which introduced an internal market into the health service, were and are promoted as increasing 'efficiency'. And discussion of the reforms is obscured by technicalities, with people saying things like, 'of course we accept the purchaser/provider divide', or 'incentives are no longer perverse'! The article by myself and Pam Smith has a go at opening up this exclusionary language. The key points are that the reforms have hugely increased the costs of running the health service, and seem to have been funded partly by a reduction in some types of care. They have greatly worsened the financial squeeze on provision, with results which Loretta Loach charts in a moving patient's-eye account.

So what of funding? How *are* we going to sustain our public services? Two ideas have dominated recent British public debate: the notion that we 'cannot afford' decent public services, and a near-phobia about tax finance. Public opinion polls consistently demonstrate support for better services, yet we have talked ourselves into a political corner, where increased tax finance has become politically unattainable. It seems that in order to fund the kind of mix we need of mutual insurance, social investment and redistribution, we are going to have to *call* the funding something other than 'tax'.

To achieve this, even to think clearly about it, we are going to have to abandon the rigid categories of 'public' and 'private', and design mixed and innovative institutions. Schemes which can combine relative equity (that is, some redistribution), low administrative costs, probity, and sufficient finance need to have as key features compulsory contributions - you must pay if you can - and an organisational form which is 'off-shore' from the public sector, yet tightly regulated and commanding public confidence.

Jane Falkingham and Paul Johnson put forward just such a scheme for pensions. Called the Unified Funded Pension System, their proposal is for a fund which combines individual compulsory pensions savings funds with tax subsidy for those with low lifetime earnings, creating a scheme to be run by heavily regulated commercial management. They argue that on this basis we *can* afford much better pensions for everyone without creating disincentives for private saving.

We face the same organisational and funding issues in health care. We spend too low a proportion of our national income on health care. To spend more, and to get the best, least divisive health service for our money, we need to find a new social finance system fast - or at least a fenced-off bit of taxation people may be persuaded to treat differently - or the NHS will be eaten away by an interaction of rising costs and piecemeal privatisation.[4]

In the process of outlining their pensions scheme, Falkingham and Johnson pick apart and explain the problems of 'means-testing' and argue that the Labour-aligned Social Justice Commission report proposals do not overcome these problems.[5] A number of articles in this issue try in this way both to explore economic technicalities in accessible language, and to come at the big economic issues of social welfare from starting points which are neither 'Old' nor 'New' Labour, but are deeply concerned with the ethics and effectiveness of 'the public'.

Which brings us to the final theme. One of the worst consequences of deep social division is the difficulty we have in hearing each other - in listening across divides. Attempts by the government systematically to devalue public 'voices' of professionals in the media and public services seem partly to have backfired (as John Clarke suggests), but have still eaten away at public dialogue, as has the assault on local government. In winding up the many voices examining the democratising of our public sphere, John Stewart offers experiences and methods for (re)learning to think collectively in public.

---

4. John Hills has recently made this argument, see J.Hills, 'Funding the welfare state', *Oxford Review of Economic Policy*, Vol. 11 No.3, Autumn 1995.
5. The Commission on Social Justice, *Social Justice: Strategies for National Renewal*, Vintage 1994.

Welfare settlements and racialising practices

Gail Lewis

*The interaction between concepts of 'race',
ethnicity and national belonging in the making and
remaking of the welfare state in Britain.*

It is half a century since the consolidation in Britain of what has become known as the welfare state and since the first of the post second world war wave of migrants from the black colonies began to arrive on these shores. During that time much has occurred to alter the terms on which those migrants turned settlers, and also the terms on which their descendants have been inserted into the welfare relations which were organised by the Beveridge reforms.

These terms have been fundamentally altered by the new 'settlements' imposed by the Thatcherite reforms. In seeking to reconfigure the relation between 'the people' and the state, the reforms reorganised the agencies and professions through which welfare was delivered. But the terms have also been altered by the struggles of black people themselves to gain equality of access to welfare services and to resist the racist practices which conditioned both their use of, and employment in, these services. As we head for the new century, and are faced with the project of imagining and struggling for a new welfare settlement organised around more inclusive forms of belonging, we need to think about the terrains upon which 'race', ethnicity and welfare have been articulated in the preceding decades.

Beveridge

It has long been accepted among all sections of the left that the creation and administration of the Beveridge welfare state in Britain represented a 'settlement' (or 'historic compromise') between capital, organised labour and the state. The components of this settlement were steady economic growth, apparently sustained by Keynesian policies with a commitment to full (male) employment, and public expenditure in key areas of welfare. Since the 1970s feminists have established that a hitherto unspoken, but nevertheless central additional component of this settlement was a familial ideology in which the normative family form was that of male breadwinner, dependent housewife, and their children.

However only since the 1980s has there has been a gradual, wider acceptance that deeply embedded in the conceptualisation and practice of the Beveridge welfare reforms there was also a notion of the nation, and with it one of 'race'.

Universalism and equality

Alongside these dominant aspects of the 'settlement' was another: that of universalism. Universalism in this context is to be understood in at least two senses. There is the sense inherited from the Fabian roots of much social policy, that the welfare state must be concerned with providing services and benefits for all rather than seeking to provide on a selective basis. Universal in this sense entails meeting need as need arises, a part of the contract between state, employer and worker which was encoded in the system of national insurance contributions.

A quite different notion of universalism emerged however in the actual delivery of diverse welfare services and benefits emanating from a plethora of agencies. As Catherine Jones pointed out in an examination of the relation between black people and social policy, in those areas of the welfare state which had a remit for the entire population - national insurance, national health and education - the brand of universalism was defined by varying notions of equality.[1] In national insurance, equality was about treatment, while in health it was about equality of access and effectiveness, and in education (which was of course compulsory) universality was linked to the pursuit of equality of opportunity.

---

1. Catherine Jones, *Immigrants and Social Policy*, London, Tavistock, London 1977.

Meanwhile, alongside these areas of provision were others which were never intended to be used by all or most of the population, such as housing and national assistance. There emerged therefore a potential distinction between the users of the more properly universal services, such as education and health, and those who also used the other *de facto* more selective services. Hence, the different meanings of universality and equality became attached to diverse constituencies of welfare recipients, and through this process, welfare carried the means of differentiation among them.

The welfare consensus which was articulated in the Beveridge reforms therefore already carried the seeds from which would be generated boundaries of inclusion/exclusion around notions of 'race', nation and/or ethnicity. This became apparent almost immediately since the implementation of this welfare state was accompanied by the arrival and settlement of people from the (ex)colonies. For these groups 'race' was the marker of differentiation around which exclusions were effected, but what 'race' signified was neither static nor uncontested.

As a consequence, in charting the history of welfare exclusion and marginality it is also possible to narrate a history of the reconstitution of the 'coloured immigrant' into her/his contemporary position as 'ethnic minority'. In doing so one would also be considering the ways in which this shift accompanied a recognition of the permanency of settlement of commonwealth migrants. Nevertheless each moment in the history involved a replay of a constitution of difference organised around 'racial' or ethnic signifiers. In this way black people's welfare needs and use was constructed as an essentialised particularity, measured against a de-ethnicised but 'white' universal which was treated as the norm.

The 'solution' of bussing

That the presence of black populations within Britain was seen as a problem of colour and nationhood which had to be managed early on can be seen in the field of education in general and the incidence of 'bussing' in particular. In 1963 the Commonwealth Immigrants Advisory Council (CIAC) recommended in the draft of its second report to the Home Office that school catchment areas should, 'where necessary', be adjusted to ensure a 'racial' balance.[2] Where such adjustment was

---

2. Published as *Second Report of Commonwealth Immigrants Advisory Council*, Cmnd 2266, HMSO, London 1964.

not sufficient to ensure the appropriate degree of dispersal of 'immigrant' children then bussing should be implemented.

The concern in official circles about 'immigrant' children in English schools was echoed amongst some sections of the white parent population. In Southall some such parents began to complain to their local education authority about the 'swamping' of local primary schools by 'immigrant' children. Their agitation resulted in the LEA sending a delegation to the then Minister of Education, Sir Edward Boyle, who in October of 1963 visited Southall in an attempt to 'reassure' and calm the local white population. Further evidence that the general welfare consensus enshrined in the Beveridge reforms was accompanied by a 'settlement' on a discourse of race is provided by the fact that the incoming Labour government of 1964 reaffirmed the commitment to a policy of dispersal. This reaffirmation was contained in the (in)famous Circular 7/65 (*The Education of Immigrants*), and again in the White Paper on *Immigration from the Commonwealth*.

I n the terms of this racial discourse, national integration in the face of the black presence could only be achieved if an upper limit of 33 per cent 'immigrant' pupil presence in any one school was maintained. The concern for the integrative effects of welfare had been a major concern of the Fabians for whom such 'integration' was centred on class divisions. But since ideas of 'race' and nation both underwrote Fabian socialism and were embedded in the Beveridge reforms, it was an easy jump to rearticulate the idea of integration to the presence of populations differentiated around 'racial' and/or cultural signifiers. Official discourse and policy and white parental 'fear' represented just such a shift but this did not mean that all LEAs adopted a policy of dispersal. Even so Townsend, in research carried out for the DES, found that 11 out of 33 authorities surveyed were in fact operating a such a policy including Ealing (which covered Southall), Bradford and Blackburn.[3]

What this story of 'bussing' in Britain demonstrates is the ways in which a settlement on 'race' and ethnicity was reached in one field of welfare. This had the effect of producing a racialising discourse in which the presence of black children in 'English' schools was constructed as a problem because they represented an erosion of what was seen as English homogeneity. As Boyle was to say in an

---

3. H.E.R. Townsend, *Immigrant Pupils in England: The LEA Response*, NFER, Slough 1971.

interesting and inverted use of colonial discourse:

> ... the opportunities children have in their homes for learning and gaining knowledge of England can be very unequal; and just as they can be unequal as between native children ... so there are greater inequalities of opportunity between native children and immigrant children... [for this reason] efforts must be made to prevent individual schools from becoming immigrant schools... [and] ... one must recognise the reasonable fear of many parents that their children will get less than a fair share of the teachers' attention when a great deal of it must of necessity be given to both language teaching and to the social training of immigrant children.[4]

'Ethnicity' and welfare

This early example from education shows that the black presence required an adjustment in the terms of the welfare settlement. We can glimpse the ways in which the erstwhile immigrants became distilled into essential ethnic subjects in another site of welfare policy and practice - that of the personal social services in the 1980s. By now black populations had been positioned within a discourse of 'ethnic minority'. The forms of exclusion and marginalisation from a normalised universal notion of 'need' were structured through this discourse, since 'normal' need was not an ethnic one.

Kobena Mercer has pointed out that

> term 'ethnic minority' ... connotes the black subject as a minor, an abject, childlike figure necessary for the legitimation of paternalistic ideologies of assimilation and integration that underpinned the strategy of liberal multiculturalism.[5]

The rise of 'ethnicity' as the predominant mode through which Britain's increasing multicultural population was articulated in British official and popular discourse had the effect of positioning those defined as 'ethnic minorities' as 'in' but not 'of' Britain/England. 'They' may be permanently 'here' but by casting them as culturally different and minor they were still constituted as 'other'. Ethnic belongingness continued to be tied to notions of what it is to be 'English/British', with all those whose ethnic ascription and/or identity was outside of this spatial, political and

---

4. *Hansard*, vol. 685 1963-64, Nov.25 - 6 Dec.
5. '"1968": Periodising Politics and Identity', in *Welcome to the Jungle*, 1994, p295.

cultural 'imagined community' being subject to racialisation.

However the shift from 'immigrant' to 'ethnic minority' was accompanied by another struggle over the terms of the 'settlement' around ethnicity / 'race' within the welfare services. Black welfare users and professionals fought for inclusion in the development of policy and delivery of services. There was indeed much to struggle about, given the discursive and practical forms of exclusion which they had faced since initial arrival. However what I want to consider here is not the legitimacy of the claims for inclusion, but rather the discursive terrain on which such inclusion was sought. I will do so by considering social work, whose record on racial matters was the subject of much interrogation by black practitioners. Inclusion, here, was sought by taking on and inverting existing understandings of 'race' and ethnicity.

Take for example social work literature. Here much of the concern with 'racial'/ethnic difference has focused on how to ensure that the needs of 'ethnic minority' clients are met. Until very recently the predominant assumption has been that the 'black/white' divide equals the 'client/social worker' one. Given that, the key issue was defined as ensuring that in areas of high 'ethnic minority' populations, social work staff could become equipped to deal with clients whose needs were defined by 'race' or ethnicity and were therefore 'different' by definition from the 'normal' social services client. 'Racial' or ethnic belongingness is not seen as something applicable to all people, so it is not a field of ethnic differences that is conceptualised but a difference from the otherwise universal structuring of need which is carried by the 'usual' social services subject.

Such a conceptualisation of the issues resulted in two key and inter-related strategies to address them. There was the 'ethnic sensitivity' model in which white social workers would be trained to be 'ethnically sensitive' by learning the codes and rules of ethnic minority cultures. Accompanying this was the 'black social workers' model which aimed at recruiting people from these 'ethnic' communities to social work courses and social services departments. Such 'ethnic' social workers would provide a sort of in-house resource for white social workers, offering them an insight into 'the cultural background of their black clients, their life-styles, their norms and values, their use of words, the "do's and don'ts" of relating to other cultures'.[6]

---

6. Basil Manning, 'The Black Social Worker', in Ahmed, Cheetham and Small (eds.), *Social Work with Black Children and their Families*, London 1979.

Such an approach constitutes black social workers as essentialised ethnic subjects, albeit subjects who have a lot to offer contemporary social services departments. For in this perspective, ethnicity can only be 'decoded' by 'insiders' who will then 'translate' it for 'outsiders'. The meanings which attach to ethnicity or ethnic belongingness are treated as self-evident, unquestionable and certainly uncontested. This is especially so in the context of 'cultural misunderstanding' which is assumed to be a major problem facing social services departments and their staff. 'Cultural misunderstanding' derives from 'cultural barriers' which are both 'natural' and immutable. Such an approach was to become condensed around that quintessential signifier of ethnic difference 'the Asian woman'.

The 'Asian woman' and the racialisation of need

In the context of social work, and indeed many other state organised welfare institutions, this signifier has a particular sharpness because it condenses the links between women and the family, and it is both women and families who form the main user base/target of social services. This linkage has provided the context for an articulation of ethnic theories of the 1970s to 1980s/90s social work theory and practice. For example in a book on social work in multi-ethnic Britain published in the late 1980s the authors cite the work of Roger Ballard as a good practice guide to understanding 'Asian families'.[7]

> Whites often believe South Asian family life to be too constricting. If an Indian or Pakistani woman is in conflict with her parents or husband, an outsider may assume that the subordinate role which South Asian women are expected to play towards their fathers and husbands … is at the root of the problem … such an interpretation may be partially correct, but the woman would be unlikely to be seeking to alter her situation fundamentally. To do so would be to reject a major part of the cultural values of her own ethnic group. Her complaint is, in practice, much more likely to be about the particular behaviour of her own husband or father, measured not in terms of her own standards, but those of her own group.

This offers a powerful example of the links made between racialised or ethnicised commonsense about black populations and the construction of an understanding

---

7. Ely and Denny (1987), *Social Work in a Multi-Racial Society*, Gower, London, p86.

about the needs of such populations. Black feminists have long critiqued essentialising constructions of 'the Asian woman' and Nasir has recently made this point well in relation to social policy.[8] For my argument what is salient about this approach is that whilst its stated aim is to ensure equality of service delivery, it does so in a way which reproduces and strengthens the racial, cultural, gendered and professional hierarchies which have been central organising principles in both the pre and post Thatcherite welfare state.

Black professionals in social services

That this is so is not however simply the result of the imposition of what some might want to call 'white values'. Many developments in social services and professional thinking in social work are the result of struggles of black professionals within this field to influence policy development and practice. This has been particularly influential in the highly politicised field of adoption and fostering policy. Just as the 'Asian Woman' became a sign of essentialised ethnic difference and 'otherness', the issue of transracial adoption and fostering became a site of intense struggle over the meaning and policy implications of ethnic diversity.

What the history of the transracial adoption debate makes clear is that white policy makers, managers and practitioners were not alone in viewing 'race' and ethnicity as fixed, essential categories. Thus it is possible to trace a convergence between New Right discourses on 'race' and what Gilroy has called ethnic absolutist ideas in statements emerging from sections of professional welfare workers.[9] This has been most clearly and forcefully presented in writings from the Association of Black Social Workers and Allied Professionals (ABSWAP) which became fairly powerful in the 1980s.

This is a complicated story. It holds many lessons for those wishing to imagine a newly refigured welfare regime which recognised and resisted racism but which did not organise its structures and professional practices around essentialist notions of 'race', ethnicity and national belonging. For example it is clear from reports of the

---

8. S. Nasir, '"Race", Gender and Social Policy', in C. Hallett (ed), *Women and Social Policy: An Introduction*, Harvester Wheatsheaf, Hemel Hempstead 1996; and see also P. Parmar, 'Young Asian Women: A Critique of the Pathological Approach', in *Multiracial Education*, vol.9 no.3, summer 1981.
9. Paul Gilroy, *There Ain't No Black in the Union Jack*, Hutchinson, London 1987.

founding conference of ABSWAP held in 1980 that part of the motivation for the organisation was to reveal, confront and undermine the explicit and implicit racism in much social work policy and practice. As such ABSWAP was part of a much wider tide of black activism aimed at fighting racism. This had the effect of challenging existing hegemonic notions of culture and identity.

In this context (which was also that of a second tide of municipal socialism) ABSWAP did some important work in challenging the myth of the pathological black (Caribbean) family and in revealing the practice implications of the discursive underpinnings of policy. For example John Small, the organisation's first president writes:

> the dominant construct [of the individual in society which operates in social work] excludes the black experience ... Consequently, concepts, definitions of situations and descriptions of events are seen purely from a white perspective ... Operating within this framework, the social worker uses professional techniques to bring the individual or family into line with the built-in assumptions and values of the dominant constructs...[10]

This statement is double-edged for, while it highlights the links between discourse and practice, it also has another effect. What is interesting about the formulation of this statement is its suggestion that there is an inherent opposition between 'black' and 'white' perspectives and experiences. For Small then, as for Ballard, there are fixed 'black' and 'white' experiences, understandings and perceptions of 'self'.

According to this perspective the purported dissonance between 'black' and 'white' conceptions has most profound effects in identity formation and it was on these terms that ABSWAP launched a major attack on transracial fostering and adoption policy. Certainly there was much to question about local authority policy in this area since it was often the case that black families were dismissed as automatically unsuitable as fosters and adopters. Similarly children of two black or mixed parentage were (and are) over-represented in the registers of children put forward for long term fostering or adoption. In this sense notions of black familial pathology acted to preclude diversification in the range of potential fosterers and/ or adopters. The 'Soul Kids' Campaign in Lambeth from 1976, and the

---

10. John Small, 'Towards a Black Perspective in Social Work: A Transcultural Exploration', in M. Langan and P. Lee (eds), *Radical Social Work Today*, Unwin Hyman, London 1989.

mushrooming of similar schemes aimed at finding black families to join local authority registers of foster carers and adoptors, had some effect in undermining notions of the pathological black family.

But it is a long way from recognising the effects of racism on both social work and psychiatric practice to arguing that a 'healthy' self image and an 'integrated' identity is reducible to the single issue of 'race', or indeed to arguing that 'black' and 'white' are fixed binary opposites. Tizard and Phoenix have made the point that such a position denies heterogeneity and division within black communities along lines of gender, age, social class or place of upbringing at the same time as it constructs a fixed divide between 'black' and 'white'.[11]

Nevertheless the ABSWAP position was sufficiently influential that by the end of the 1980s a new orthodoxy had emerged regarding the issue of transracial adoption and most local authority social services departments had adopted a 'same-race' placement policy for adoption and fostering. I would argue that ABSWAP was able to achieve this influence because they mapped their concerns and perspectives onto an already fertile terrain. By the time that they launched their intervention the black presence in Britain had already been discursively refigured as 'ethnic minorities', a shift from the earlier positioning as 'immigrants'. This reconstitution made possible belief in a particularity of need which derived directly from ethnic or racial essentials. This marked off these groups from the 'universal' needs associated with the white clients for whom service delivery was predominantly designed. Given this, it was not too radical a step to impose a policy prescription which was based on assumptions that 'black needs' could only be met by black providers.

'New ethnicities' for new settlements

> We still have a great deal of work to do to decouple ethnicity, as it functions in the dominant discourse, from its equivalence with nationalism, imperialism, racism and the state, which are the points of attachment around which a distinctive British or, more accurately, English ethnicity have been constructed ... [but] which, because it is hegemonic, does not represent itself as an ethnicity at all.[12]

11. B. Tizard and A. Phoenix, 1993, Black, White or Mixed Race, London:Routledge.
12. Stuart Hall, 'New Ethnicities', reprinted in J. Donald and A. Rattansi, *'Race', Culture and Difference*, Sage, London 1992, p257.

So far I have suggested that the 'settlements' around notions of 'race', ethnicity and national belonging contained within the welfare state since its inception have undergone a transition. In rather stark terms what I mean by this is that black people in the form of 'immigrants' have stopped being 'done to' (as in bussing). For example, they have emerged as combatative yet influential forces in a renegotiation of the terms of inclusion in some sites of welfare delivery (in the form of 'ethnic minority' professionals). Despite this transition I have contended that both forms of 'settlement' have been equally racialising. In the later model 'race'/ethnicity is accorded a foundational status structuring all experience and producing a set of racially or ethnically determined needs.

How then to imagine a reconstituted welfare state which is simultaneously anti-racist yet avoids fixing black people in racialising social practices? This is of course the stuff of politics and the means by which it can be achieved cannot be determined prior to the engagement in struggle. However such struggle does need to begin from the premise that a new politics of belonging must reformulate the dominant meanings attached to 'race' and ethnicity, whether these meanings emerge from the radical right or the nationalist left of black politics. What we must aim for is a rejection of a politics of anti-racism which closes off the possibility of shared understandings, correspondences of experience, or fluidity of identities across group boundaries.

Stuart Hall has referred to this as the constitution of 'new ethnicities'. As he says, what this means is both a disarticulation of ethnicity from notions of 'race' and nation and also a recognition that everyone speaks from within a particular culture, place or experience. For welfare this will mean a recognition that particularity of need is not something which only black people have, but white also. It will mean recognising the heterogeneity of all groups of 'service users', white as well as black. It will mean recognising that 'universality' in welfare policy must mean constructing a universality of opportunity and access whilst mediating particularity of position and need.

Women Building Bridges
A MOBILE DISPLAY

Soundings readers will already be familiar with Cynthia Cockburn's photo-narratives that have appeared in the last two issues of *Soundings*. These presented examples of women's cross-communal initiatives in N. Ireland and in Bosnia-Hercegovina.

They raise questions about the possibilities and difficulties of forging alliances across ethnic divisions despite the bitter animosities of war. Is it possible to affirm and welcome 'difference' when one identity seeks to banish another? What are the minimum requirements for working together? What has being a women got to do with it?

The two articles, and a third on Israel (to be included in the next issue of Soundings), are the basis of a photographic exhibition, *Women Building Bridges*, that has been displayed at the University of Greenwich and is due to be shown at events in Zagreb and Toronto.

The display is mounted on thirteen vertical panels of A1 size (594mm x 841mm), requiring approximately a 12 metre run of wallspace. It is available on loan free of charge. If you have a suitable venue and would like to discuss the possibility of borrowing it, your enquiry would be very welcome. Please contact:

C. Cockburn, Dept. of Sociology, City University, London EC1V 0HB. Fax: 0171 482 5670

Lipman-Miliband Trust
John Saville Award

In April 1996 the labour and social historian **John Saville** celebrated his 80th birthday. In recognition of his contributions to the labour and socialist movement and his lifetime of active political involvement, the **Lipman-Miliband Trust** has decided to make a once-off special award of £3000 to be known as the **John Saville Award**. The successful application will be for a project that reflects one or more aspects or interests of John Saville's life - as an economic, social, labour, diplomatic and oral historian, co-founder of the British New Left and of the *Socialist Register*, campaigner for academic freedom, and as an active and committed socialist.

For more information contact:
The John Saville Award, c/o Journal of Historical Studies in Industrial Relations, Keele University, Staffordshire ST5 5BG, UK.
The closing date for applications is 31 December 1996.

A race against time:

Change and the public service in the 'New South Africa'

Francie Lund

A personal account of the struggle to transform
South Africa's racially divided welfare services

South Africa had its first democratic election in April 1994. The intellectual left, in and out of exile, and in and out of universities, were strong on analysis and critique, but inexperienced about planning for and constructing the new country. International isolation meant few had learned familiarity with big systems of reform, or of how to translate policies into implementable plans. The ANC in exile had more diplomatic missions in foreign countries than the apartheid government had consulates or embassies. It had, however and of course, limited experience of actual government.

The account that follows relates a number of stories about the transition. They contain deep tragedy and deep farce. They mix the personal and the political. They point to mixes between the public and the private. The account draws from two work experiences, one before and one after the elections. In 1990 I had undertaken a survey of the state welfare services delivered by the seventeen different 'states' of the apartheid regime. In September 1994 I was recruited to be a part of the Strategic Management Team (SMT) of Health and Welfare in one of the nine new provinces, the North West. The North West comprised former Bophuthatswana, one of the four black 'states' which took independence, and the former western Transvaal, the heartland of white right wing thinking.[1]

The chief task of the SMTs was to unify the formerly racially fragmented public sector. They had been set up after the elections to be vehicles for the management of transition in the civil service. They were one of a number of mechanisms used by the new government to create spaces for the participation of people from outside government in governmental change. To the extent that one could have been prepared for this kind of task, the 1990 research helped.

The 1990 survey had resulted from a series of meetings I attended the year before. Above-ground, 'struggle politics' in the field of social policy was organised in sectors. During one week in 1989 I went to meetings on three consecutive evenings on health, education, and welfare respectively. People were beginning to plan for reconstruction, and beginning to face the reality that there might be delivery problems in meeting the demands of the Freedom Charter - for free housing, education, health for all. Where would the resources be for translating rights into real delivery? The Defence Budget of the apartheid regime was massive; all sectors now turned to its reduction to release money for primary health care, for primary schools, for welfare facilities. By the third meeting the penny dropped for me - we didn't have the remotest idea of what we were talking about. Not only did we not know about the cost of universal provision; we also didn't know about what services were being delivered in the fragmented bits of states which had been created over the past forty years.

The seventeen administrations that I visited in 1990 - five thousand miles of travelling - fell into four clusters. There were racially separate central government departments for coloured, for Indian and for white people. The vast majority of South Africans were classified black. So, next, there were departments in each of the four provinces to deliver welfare services to black South Africans in 'white South Africa'. Then there were the ten bantustans for black South Africans. Four of these had taken so-called independent status - Bophuthatswana, Ciskei, Transkei and Venda. Some 8 million South Africans there had been dispossessed of South African citizenship. Finally, six 'self-governing territories' were supposed to be preparing themselves for independence. These were Gazankulu, Kangwane, KwaNdebele, KwaZulu, Lebowa and QwaQwa.

---

1. The apartheid system was based on a system of classification of the population into four 'races' or 'population groups', which then determined one's life chances in a fundamental way. My use of the terms here does not signify any acceptance of the construct 'race'. The article could not be written without reference to the racial naming, however.

The fragmented 'governments' developed their own histories and identities. None of the ten was geographically whole: KwaZulu had about 24 different bits, but all reasonably close together. Bophuthatswana had only a few bits, but one of these was a good four hundred miles away from the others. KwaNdebele was within daily commuting distance of the economic engine of South Africa, the Johannesburg-Pretoria complex. Distant Venda was far from any major city. A large part of former KwaZulu was in functional terms part of Natal's Durban metropolitan region.

The 1990 survey: distances, capitals and coups

Finding one's way physically around this vindictive patchwork quilt was a challenge. It was easy to get to the welfare departments for the three non-African races, and for African people in 'white South Africa', since they were in major cities. The six homelands and four 'independent states' posed more of a problem.

Umtata was a comfortable shambling wide-streeted colonial small town which was later developed as the capital of Transkei. I knew it well, and it was easy to find. Lebowa and KwaNdebele, which had been excised from the Transvaal, were the most difficult, since they had been cartographically disadvantaged, so to speak, on most standard road maps by having the enlarged inset of Pretoria-Johannesburg superimposed on them. Venda and Gazankulu could be found on maps, probably because they had elements of a tourist attraction en route to the Kruger National Park.

There was a confusing diversity of names of places. The old white town would have one name from colonial times, the Post Office would sometimes have another, the telephone exchange name was sometimes different again, and then the 'new capital' - or converted old township - would have another, usually African, name.

Having tracked them down by phone or post or fax, finding them physically was on the whole easy. As the officials would say with humour: 'You can't miss it'. Many are beautifully located, on a hillside or plain. Ulundi (KwaZulu), Bisho (Ciskei) and Thohoyandou (Venda) are little Brasilias, far from anywhere. Town planning and the architecture of the major buildings is redolent of Albert Speer, with the main statue not being Hitler but a vast bronze wildebeest or elephant. The elephant has high sacred symbolic value to Venda people, but surely not as part of this physical design?

The whole study took place in a context of turbulence. When I interviewed in Phutaditjhaba, QwaQwa had just had a civil service strike, and in Venda my visit followed a coup. The Bisho interview was interrupted because personnel were called to an emergency meeting of the Ciskei Military Council. The day after the Umtata visit, the building in which I had conducted interviews was mortared - it was the home of the then Military Council, as well as the Department of Welfare.

'Authority' and secrecy

Bophuthatswana (or Bop for short) presented difficulties of a different sort. Mmabatho, the capital, gained momentary international fame as the site of the last attempted coup before the 1994 elections. The photograph of three white right-wing militants being executed in the street went around the world. This was the most difficult visit to set up, particularly because of bureaucratic rules about research. The communications were marked by, and seemed to be obsessed with, the word 'authority': who can give authority for a particular action, and whether one has received the authority for an action, or been delegated it.

The welfare department was in Mmabatho's new shopping complex. Social workers in the office said that the contact person, in control of my visit, was not there, and would be returning only in two days time. 'No problem', I said cheerfully, 'he must have left a list of instructions about my visit. Could you help me find who has it?' The social worker looked aghast and said it would have been she herself. 'No problem', I said, 'who is his superior? Can you take me to him or her?' I was told that that person was away also with my contact person. 'And the superior after that?' Away on leave. 'And after that?' In another department, and thus would not know about my visit at all.

I asked the social workers whether they knew the answers to my questions. 'Oh yes, certainly. We work in this area.' 'Well then', back to cheery again, 'we could talk'. 'No. We have not been delegated the authority to talk to you. We are embarrassed, and would like to talk, but we cannot.' 'Who can delegate the authority?' They recited the same, still absent, people. 'Could I go to the minister and ask him to delegate the authority to you?' 'This is a good idea,', they said, 'but it makes us vulnerable. He would then know we had already spoken to you, and we do not have the authority to speak to you.'

This 'authority' is deadly when it is combined, in all administrations, with no sensibility about the difference between public and private domains. South Africa was a very uncivil society in the sense that there was no space in which to practise how to be a normal citizen, and the civil service did not know - could not know - that there is a difference between governance and a political party. The apartheid regime was based on sinister secrecy, and was so totalitarian that officials in welfare, or health, or education, got the boundaries between public and private spheres muddled.

For example, to prepare for interviews I used a university library to borrow Estimates of Expenditure, and took copies of these along. In every single one of the seventeen administrations, officials expressed surprise, and in many cases deep suspicion, about my having them in

'The themes of wasted time, distance and displacement ran like a thread'

my possession. Most South Africans - ordinary public servants and ordinary citizens - did not know that people have a right to know what government accounts are. As serious was the fact that the most senior welfare official in most administrations could not 'read' the budget in any sensible way. Planning was ideologically, not financially driven. The ideological engine room for all this was clearly in Pretoria, the real capital of the apartheid state.

What a waste of time: working in welfare

A story which might be called 'The prisoner of Venda' captures the dangerousness and the meaninglessness of these separate administrations. On the fourth floor of a new building in Venda's capital, Thohoyandou, a social worker described how a Venda citizen who worked on a nearby white South African farm - she pointed to the farm in the distance - had murdered a fellow farm worker. He was taken to a South African court, tried, and sentenced to death. He was sent to Death Row in Pretoria Central, about 250 miles away.

His family wished to visit him. The social worker sent the application for a visit from the office where we were sitting, to a building which she pointed out - Venda's Foreign Affairs Department. Foreign Affairs sent the application to the South African Embassy building nearby. The Embassy sent the application to Pretoria Central, which sent it back to a town some 70 miles away from Thohoyandou, in South Africa. Here the application was considered by the welfare office of the region in which the crime took place. From there it went back to Pretoria, was returned the South African Embassy here, back to the Foreign Affairs Department, and from there to here in the social worker's office.

'But surely', I asked, 'by the time all this has happened, the prisoner would be hanged?' 'Exactly', she said, 'and that is why we went through the formalities of application, and then made our own informal arrangements so his family could get to see him in time.'

The fragmentation rendered the whole apartheid system opaque. As a researcher, it was exhausting keeping everything in mind. What was equivalent to what? What law governed which benefits? Which procedures were in operation? Where am I? Where are we? Social security benefits were a case in point. Social assistance was called variously Poor Relief, Relief of Distress, Social Relief, and Paupers' Rations - a Victorian relic in the highveld. But they were all governed by different procedures, and mostly, they were administered at the discretion of officials anyway. The rules regarding child maintenance allowances were chaotically different in various administrations; many of the bantustan areas did not award them at all.

I learned to track down clues to the control by Pretoria co-ordinating departments through close reading of budget line items. In several different homelands' budgets, 'Deaf and Dumb' was translated as 'Deaf and Dump'. Properly separate administrations would not have made the identical error. Almost unbelievably, four years later I would pick it up again in the North West as 'Death and Dump'.

There was an overwhelming sense of well-intentioned social workers being dragged down by time and by distance and by the meaninglessness of much of the work. The political turbulence, and the control of black people's access to towns, meant that there were built-in incentives to hide true identities, or create double identities. Social workers spent hours simply tracing people, for the juvenile courts, or for the parole courts, or for maintenance grants - people who were 'deported' to KwaNdebele, for example, in whose interest it was to keep two names and two addresses.

The themes of wasted time, distances and displacement ran like a thread through all of the visits.

Closing the distances: working with the SMT

The white civil service was part of the economic project of the former government, providing protected employment and material security for, in the first place, Afrikaans-speaking white South Africans. It was part of the deliberate strategy of building Afrikaner control, and of promoting the nationalism of 'die volk'. The bantustans then became a project to provide legitimacy with black people for this mad plan.

Well before the April 1994 elections, the Nationalist Party had realised these 'states' were on the road to nowhere, and would have to be re-integrated. As early as 1989, for example, government documents reflect the beginnings of welding uniformity in the social security systems. How to overcome the fragmentation of these diverse bits, following the 1994 elections?

E ach Department in the nine new provinces was allocated a budget to set up Strategic Management Teams (SMTs) for this purpose, and the SMTs typically employed some people outside of government to work with them, to bridge the gap between the civil servants from the previously separate administrations, and to bring in management and planning skills. The SMT which I joined in the North West comprised the three senior people in social work, social security, and administration from each of former Bop and former Transvaal. Prior to the establishment of the SMT, an independent social policy consultant who worked out of Johannesburg had been asked to start the work of integration, and she had held a number of workshops with the staff. She was then asked to be a consultant to the SMT, as was a local minister from the Dutch Reformed Church who had been playing an active bridging role between white and black welfare organisations in the Transvaal. I was brought in as the third outsider.

The provincial minister or MEC (Member of the Executive Committee) of Health and Welfare was a medical doctor and a seasoned activist. Again I heard the word 'authority', but this time with different intent. 'Use my authority to go and work as fast as possible to change things. There is a gap. It is narrow in scope, and it will be short in time. Run with it. Use my authority to change things. Don't refer everything back to me. But don't undermine my authority.'

The key objectives of the SMT were to keep a continuity of welfare services, while managing the change involved with integrating services, and developing a structure for the new unified department. The starting point for planning future services had to be a stock-taking of what was actually in the new province - how many personnel, how many places in institutions, computers, cars, offices. And, importantly, what kinds of private welfare organisations with what levels of management skills who could come in to help. Once the SMT was in place, and the stock-taking - or Situation Analysis - was completed, we were to start the process of decentralising management and control to five districts.

White people had been 'a race against time', out of touch with the modern era. Now the new South Africa was involved in a race against time to undo what had been set up. In some respects it was too late: a great deal of unilateral restructuring had been done in the four years between Mandela's release and the new government taking power. In the past there had been massive state subsidy of non-profit residential facilities for elderly white people, for example. Many of these have been sold off to the private sector, with wealthier white people being the only ones in the market.

'White people had been "a race against time", out of touch with the modern era'

A central dynamic of the SMT was that the senior civil servants would all, obviously, be competing for a reduced number of top posts. People from the different administrations had, in towns such as Rustenburg, been literally working on different sides of the same street while in different 'countries'. They led separated lives, but what they knew intimately was the relative status and size of the package attached to various civil service rankings in the different areas; they knew the equivalence of rankings even though posts might be called different names.

Another potentially divisive dynamic was language. Tswana is the first language of the vast majority of black people in the North West, and Afrikaans the first language of the vast majority of white civil servants there. Few whites have any knowledge of Tswana. Afrikaans - 'the language of the oppressor' as it used to be known - is in fact the second language of most black people there. There is deep political resistance by black people to its use in formal settings, however, such as when civil servants from former Bop and former Transvaal are meeting for the first time. English was used, but the other languages were used powerfully as a mechanism of exclusion - of one side by the other, or of both sides to exclude the outsiders - throughout the process.

The situation analysis: calling to account

The Situation Analysis made extraordinary demands on the time and energy of welfare workers. Teams, or Commissions, covered the different fields of service, such as child care, care of the aged, social security. Their mandate was at one level simple: count everything. Count people, both citizens and personnel. Count facilities: beds, laundries, playgrounds, advice centres. Count equipment: offices, telephones, computers, filing cabinets, cars. Put them on a map. And the counting must be done according to race, so that a bench mark is established, at the transition, against which to measure how effective redistribution and reallocation will be over a five year period.

There was a strong resistance to collecting information along racial lines. When we asked for it, one white person said, 'But since the elections we mustn't do this any more. Race does not matter any more.' Another complained that such racial identification would mean too much concentration on the past, whereas 'This is meant to be the new South Africa'.

The resistance was deeply relateed to not wanting to confront precisely how distorted service provision had been. When the results were coming in, we gathered to get first estimates. It was clear enough: 87 per cent of welfare spending had been going to white people who constituted less than 10 per cent of the population. One division of the former Transvaal department had eleven cars for thirteen people; the Bop department had not one car for its specific use.

One official responded, 'But this is outrageous - the figures must be wrong.'

'You did the counting. If it's wrong, go and check your sums.'

And then the shift started: 'We didn't know it was this bad.' Then, 'We are so embarrassed.' And then the important one: 'This has to change.' And, finally: 'We have to change this.'

I think that that was what the Situation Analysis was really about. It was to insist on history, and use what actually happened in material terms to measure change. It was a fundamentally unsocial-work-like way of approaching the management of change. It said, 'We won't spend very much time here on getting to know each other, on overcoming racial distances, or saying we must like each other. We have to start with understanding what apartheid really did. And future welfare planning will be built around shifting those resources in the interests of equity. It will be built on numbers.'

Towards democracy in the civil service

One objective of the change process was the decentralisation of health and welfare, driven by the new policy of establishing a District Health Systems approach. Five districts were demarcated based primarily on potential economic growth centres, and on the network of roads. Central management committees in Mmabatho were Health Management, and Welfare Management (the co-ordinating Committees), and then three which were shared by both health and welfare: Logistics, Financing, and Human Resource Development.

The starting point of practical decentralisation was to establish District Transitional Management Committees (DTMCs). On the health side, the DTMCs had begun with a process of consultation with staff in the districts. Their numbers were so large that representatives were called to the meetings. In welfare, the numbers were much smaller, and the SMT decided that all staff - social workers, social security staff, and administrative staff - should attend.

We spent one SMT meeting hammering out agreements about the structure and purpose of DTMCs. This was where the SMT members had to face that decentralisation really meant taking some authority away from them, and achieving consensus about the DTMCs was critical. The DTMCs were to be small and management oriented. While small, they would still have to be representative in an overall way of the former administrations, race, gender, and of rural and urban areas. They would be interim bodies, until such time as top posts in the districts had been advertised and filled, or until 1 April 1995 (a year after the elections), whichever was the earlier.

For the composition of the DTMCs, those on the health side of the Department comprised a nurse, a doctor, and an administrative person. In welfare we added two positions. One was for a 'junior manager' - the intention was to create a fast track option for bright young black staff who had been held down by the bureaucracy of the past. The second was to keep one space for someone from the non-governmental welfare organisations. We needed to import management skills which were in the private organisations. There was a commitment by the new government to working in partnership with civil society, and a demand from civil society organisations to participate.

The SMT then called a mass consultative meeting for personnel at which the SMT proposals for DTMCs were circulated and discussed. This was well-attended, and those present were positive, and enthused about the intended changes. My sense was that few really grasped, in that short meeting, what was about to unfold in the five district meetings at which DTMCs were to be elected - if not wholly democratically elected, then through a process of democratic nomination.

The venues provided a powerful symbolic backdrop to this path-breaking process. Sonop Settlement hosted the first meeting, in Odi district. Sonop - which means Sunrise - was set up in the 1930s for poor white bywoners (tenants) - who were being evicted from farms. The government gave them a strip of land at Sonop, so that they could be productive and self-reliant, and not dependent on the state. Over the years various services were added, and it came to admit mostly 'multi-problem families'. The small town and adjoining land is now a total institution with schools, training workshops, facilities for frail elderly, for pre-school care, and so on. Black people have been there in a service capacity. It is a telling example of the Nationalist political patronage and welfare statism for whites only of the last government, with its R11 million annual state subsidy.

The five meetings were attended by between 60 and 120 people each. On the whole the group was representative of the provincial population profile, with about eight black people to each white person. People did not know each other across administrations, or across work types. We designed an exercise that would get people to concentrate their minds on management as the key issue of the day. The question they had to address in small informal groups was: what are the qualities which would characterise a good manager of social services or social security?

The outcome was obvious, and helpful in its obviousness - all focused on knowledge of the job, personal leadership skills, into which was lumped vision, communication, able to motivate staff, being a good role model and so on; and the element of control, authority, respect, able to discipline and so on. We then moved on to a carefully structured verbal input which followed a written handout, about the DTMCs. We were intensely aware of the need for care and for transparency - that everything about the process and the rules should be written down. This was so that people could not say they had been duped or manipulated. There were not a lot of questions about this document; some surly acceptance, or questions about provincial boundaries and district boundaries. The most criticism was evoked by the junior manager position. Opening up spaces in the career ladder is so decisively contrary to the relentlessly defined layering of bureaucracies.

We then moved on to the guidelines for elections. People were to nominate for a 'package' of people: their list of five or six people should include an administrative person, a social worker, and someone from social security. It should also include someone from the non-governmental organisations, and someone for the junior manager position. The 'package' had to bear in mind representativity in terms of former administrations, gender, race and rural-urban spread. Voting would be by secret ballot, which was a new concept for many.

The resistance was strong and deep and consistent. It ran across job categories: 'We social workers cannot vote for people in social security - we don't know them'. It ran across different administrations: 'We from former Transvaal cannot vote for former Bop people - we don't know them.' People did not want to choose. They wanted enough spaces on the DTMC that every one could remain where they were. One participant tried to argue for one person from each of six magisterial districts for each of social work, social security and administration - a 'lean and mean' management committee of eighteen!

We countered the resistance with a lobbying exercise. 'Yes it is difficult to choose when you don't know people, but we have to have DTMCs in place, so that is why we are now going to learn how to lobby. And if all the social workers here, who are in the majority, nominate only social workers, then the package will not be representative, and the MEC will override you and choose for you. But he cannot know as well as you, at this point, who the best potential interim managers in welfare are. You have an opportunity to choose who will lead you, locally, through this transition.'

It was at this point in each meeting that one could spot the people - wide-eyed and open-mouthed - who finally grasped that what was going on was radical,

'wide-eyed, open-mouthed, people finally grasped that what was going on was radical, and seriously intended'

was seriously intended, and that their views were going to be taken seriously. It represented an opportunity to take control of their own working lives to some extent, in a small way.

We explained there would be few rules. One was that no-one could leave the room to escape the process; two was that people should move around fast and actively, and not settle into desultory groups. If one or two large groups formed which were dominated by one or two high talkers, these would be broken up as power blocs. People should understand that the lobbying was a collective exercise, a way of getting and giving as much information, and exerting influence, as possible, in a short time. We would thereafter go to the nomination process, which was about individual private decisions by secret vote.

Then: Ready, Steady, Go. There was a slightly disbelieving silence of three or four seconds, followed by a roar of noise and energy and action. It was exhilarating. It was risky territory. No training course I knew could have prepared one fully. But it was deeply satisfying to be a part of trying to institutionalise the democratic process.

Assessment? It's too early to tell

The meeting to decentralise management in the Vryburg region took part towards the end of the process. This is the far west of the province, and it is where rich (white) cattle ranching territory must be re-integrated with the most undeveloped part of former Bop. The municipal board at the entry to the town announces: 'Welcome to Vryburg, the Texas of South Africa'. I was told that farmers until recently came to town on Saturdays on horseback, gun in holster, swastika-like logo of the white right wing para-military organisation on sleeve.

On the drive from Vryburg back to Mmabatho, there was a dramatic thunderstorm to the north of the sunshine and blue sky. The rain was falling at one end of the cloud, and at the other end of the dark purple and grey sweep, a dust devil created a spiral of earth going up as if it was joining the cloud. Tom Waites was singing, 'Small Change got rained on with his own 38'. And I think, yes my soul, maybe you're the cowgirl in Texas. This is very risky stuff. Too dramatic.

The chance of the intervention being sustainable worries me very much. *Plus ça change?* Will anything stick? It might all be purely romantic. How helpful, really, can temporary outside consultants be in the process of change in large bureaucracies? And though the SMTs and other policy bodies have encouraged private participation in state activities, there is justified criticism that it is a small, elitist circle which has been involved. This has not been about the engagement of the masses in policy-making and change that the pre-election rhetoric promised.

For real reasons of public accountability, there are ways in which state bureaucracies must work slowly, cannot be visionary. The Nationalist Party had forty-eight years to drive people apart, to use the machinery of government to control, to divide, to rule. After all the waste of time that apartheid was, the SMTs had to work at terrifying speed. One imperative driving the pace was that the new Estimates of Expenditure had to be prepared on time - the budgetary calendar is impervious to the lack of experience of the new governors, insists that the budgets are in, regardless of whether they are based on the goals of the new government. The other was that the chance of change depended to some extent on the element of surprise. This was especially important in preventing the old (black and white) bureaucratic guard from digging in their heels and entrenching their separate positions.

I t would be pretty senseless to strive, yet, for any objective assessment of this intervention, this attempt to change. There was honesty of purpose. But the speed occasioned casualties: deeply hurtful experiences for some people, bred of misunderstanding, of discounting really different histories, of not enough time to listen.

The spaces for participation in the new government appear to be closing slowly, as things settle down, and it is 'business as usual'. Government is still too big, at provincial and at central level, and the lack of skills, in accounting and management, available in the new government is cause for deep concern. The effects of apartheid's denial of education and opportunity will take years to overcome.

At a simple level, a concrete product of the SMT was the report - the Situation Analysis - which is an audit of welfare at the beginning of 'the new South Africa'. Getting the numbers right was a necessary condition for being able to make an assessment of change in the coming years. Perhaps an indicator of change will be whether the report is used in future planning and evaluation. Or, better, if the new management team, without the intervention of outsiders, did its own new report soon.

All those involved will have their own stories about the journey. My partial account is incomplete and is written with regard for the people involved. Other, and different, accounts and assessments will have to wait. It is too early to tell.

Perverse Incentives:

An NHS notebook

Maureen Mackintosh and Pam Smith

The NHS reforms have brought some expensive forms of competition into the cash-limited health service, and have created some curious incentives, not least for increasing costs, and for 'treatment not care'. Maureen Mackintosh and Pam Smith have been keeping a notebook.

Incentives and the NHS

Quotations and events

Commentary

'Until very recently the public services ran on perverse incentives and without any bottom line.... there was no reward for good performance and no sanctions for poor performance. The result was that there was simply no motivation for people to do better. Markets offer real incentives; they reward success and they penalise failure...In the NHS,

Eric Caines, now Professor of Health Services Management at Nottingham University, was personnel director of the NHS 1990-April 1993, through the early process of reform, so he should know what they thought they were doing. His summary of the central idea of the NHS reforms is quite clear: to create a market in order to give people the incentives to 'do better'.

the managed market was created in
an attempt once again to bring
pressure to bear for better use of
resources.'
Eric Caines, *The Health Summary* 1995, p8

We have watched over the last few years as the language of incentives, sanctions
and rewards has become embedded in political thinking on public policy. The
discourse of incentives has become associated with 'reality', with an absence of
naivety: watch how the above quotation moves quickly to associate motivation
with incentives, and 'real' incentives with markets and material rewards. The
previous or non-market NHS *had* incentives, but they were not 'real' and were
also 'perverse', a word redolent of obstinacy, improper behaviour, facing in the
wrong direction.

This is a notebook of short tales about 'perverse incentives'. It is a powerful
phrase, that. It has a precise technical meaning: it means a financial incentive
to act in a way which runs against the objectives of the institution where you
work - or indeed against what you know is right. And it has - as just suggested -
other layers of meaning, which denigrate by association worlds where the
incentive structures are not properly 'aligned', that is, where it is not clear who
has the (financial) interest in doing what. In particular, it is used, as above, to
tar the 'old' NHS with inefficiency and ineptitude, and to imply, as Caines does,
that markets are sorting the problems out.

But the situation is not as simple as that. It is *not* that the 'old' NHS had no
inefficiences: who could think that? (Yet somehow, these days, one cannot
talk about the new NHS of 'managed markets' unless one first protests
that one is not idealising the old system.) Instead, the notebook illustrates the
way that the new, reformed NHS, where governmental 'purchasers' and GPs buy
health care for all of us, is itself full of 'perverse incentives'. Though it has - as
we will also show - desirable new incentives too. But, perhaps most of all, we
want to suggest that financial incentives have come to matter more than before
in what people do. In terms of Eric Caines' meaning of 'incentives' we are now
more 'incentive-driven'. That may make incentives more real. It is not clear it
makes health care more 'efficient': indeed the meaning of efficiency is one of
the problems we consider here.

Raising or lowering costs?

Ms Primarolo: 'To ask the Secretary of State for Health what estimates her Department has made of the annual cost of negotiating and managing NHS contracts.'
Dr Mawhinney: 'None'.

Written parliamentary answer 15.7.95 quoted in *Health Care UK* 1994/5 p6

It is one of the most striking facts of the NHS reforms that a government which, in most fields, is only too anxious to cost activity, and to evaluate it in financial terms, has steadfastly refused to collect information on the cost of 'marketising' the health service.

There are two different - but in principle compatible - things that we might mean by Eric Caines' 'better use of resources': doing things more cheaply; and doing different and more desirable things. It is fair to say that the NHS reforms were supposed to do both. The reforms separated 'purchasers' of health care (local health authorities and GPs) who held the NHS budgets, from 'providers' (hospitals, ambulance services, district nursing services, GPs, all organised as autonomous contractors to the service) who bid to them for contracts to provide us all with health care. (Yes, we know GPs are in both those lists: we come back to that below!)

This 'market' framework was supposed to drive down over-all costs, because providers - it was hoped - would compete with each other for contracts by reducing their prices. At the same time, it was supposed to ensure services were more responsive to patients' needs, because it was thought that the purchasers would concentrate on identifying and buying care for those needs - undistracted by the problems of running services. In the jargon, services would be 'purchaser-led' not 'provider-led': run for us, not for the convenience of hospitals.

So let us start with the central theme of the reform: costs. Have the reforms reduced them? Do they provide *incentives* to reduce them? To tackle those seemingly straightforward questions, we need to define what we are talking about. The key argument is about *unit costs*, that is, how much it costs to treat individual patients with particular ailments. If you treat more people for the same money (increased 'throughput' as it is unsuitably called) unit costs have come down. Unfortunately, the statistics are a minefield.

'New figures from the government's statistical service show that in the past year alone, NHS hospitals treated an extra 455,000 patients. That is a 4.7 per cent increase.'

Virginia Bottomley, then Secretary of State for Health, Hansard, 25.11.94

These are not people! The numbers refer to 'finished consultant episodes' and completed day cases. Each time you see a consultant, that is an 'episode'. NHS trust hospitals are paid by the 'episode'. Measured episodes have certainly risen, but we do not know how much of that is more patients seen, and how much is counting one person several times.

'Hospitals are getting better at identifying activity. It's really a specious justification for demanding more money.'

Health authority manager, 1996 (interview with authors)

A trust hospital finance director realised she could boost out-patient numbers by ten per cent by adding in attendances at hearing aid clinics. 'Our performance appeared to have improved dramatically and the purchasers were delighted with us. Nothing had changed of course.'

Julia Drown, Guardian, 24.4.96

Hospitals do respond to purchasers' pressures to raise 'throughput' by counting 'episodes' more carefully. That increases their money in one year. It doesn't raise the total sum available to the health service, however, it just redistributes it at higher administrative cost. And, as Julia Drown went on to point out, it gets harder over time to find ways to show an upward trend.

Purchasers look for falling prices each year, when trusts renegotiate their contracts. This is part of so-called 'efficiency savings'. If trusts can find a trick to increase apparent throughput, they have reduced their price per unit without sacking staff. We have therefore given our health 'providers', such as hospitals, a strong incentive to use their resources to count their activity minutely, and to push people through the system as fast as possible.

'Throughput' has certainly risen since the reforms - and was rising before them. The average length of stay in hospital fell from 11 days in 1989 to 8 in 1994[1], but most of that drop came from increases in day cases, where people come in in the morning and leave in the evening.[2] We do not know if this apparent rise in 'efficiency' is all gain for patients. If people leave too soon, they may be more likely to be readmitted. But we do not know if readmissions are rising: the 'government statistical service', as just noted, doesn't track *people*.

Against this pressure to (appear to) reduce costs per case, we have to set the costs of managing the reformed system.

'The amount of paperwork has increased dramatically over the past year, which takes time away from client contact'

A health visitor

'The amount of paperwork has become ridiculous, some managers think it should take precedence over patient care.'

A district nurse[3]

These (representative) quotations, from a study done over 1991-1994, reflect the increase in paperwork experienced by nursing staff in both the hospital and community sectors. The increase seems to be particularly felt by those working in community care.

Ask people in the NHS what is the worst aspect of the reforms, and many will say either 'paperwork' or 'bureaucracy'. What we have done in effect is introduce into the health service a *billing system* which it previously did not need. Have you been asked your postcode recently by a hospital? Have you been told apologetically that you need a GP letter now for each visit for recurrent treatment? How much does all this additional paperwork cost? And where is the money coming from?

---

1. OHE (Office of Health Economics), *Compendium of Health Service Statistics*, 1995. The huge long term drop in length of stay in hospital reflects changing clinical practice.
2. Radical Statistics Health Group, 'NHS "indicators of success"; what do they tell us?' *British Medical Journal*, 22.4.95, pp1045-50.
3. Both quotations from M. Traynor and B. Wade, *The morale of nurses working in the community*, NHS Trust Series Report III, Daphne Heald Research Unit, Royal College of Nursing 1994.

As Dawn Primarolo MP confirmed, the government does not (want to) know how much it costs. Numbers of NHS general and senior managers went up from 4639 in 1989 to 17,900 in 1992, and continued to rise. The Audit Commission - a government body which audits the NHS - has added up higher level management costs, and come up with a figure of about £900m or 4 per cent of total NHS expenditure.[4] Adding in junior finance and clerical staff brought it up to £2.3bn. or 10.5 per cent of total current spending - and this doesn't include the increase in nurses' paperwork. Everyone agrees administration and management costs have risen fast with the reforms; no one knows how fast. A Labour opposition health spokesman offered a guesstimate of £1.5bn.as the administrative costs of the reforms, which is 3.8 per cent of NHS 1994 expenditure.[5]

The government fluctuates between claiming the cost increases are justified by previous under-management, and declaring wars on bureaucracy (including 'reclassifying' people designated managers back into professional categories).[6] Trust hospital managers agree the reforms are expensive: one estimated the additional costs of finance staff and auditing alone for one hospital at £150,000 a year, plus another £40,000 for the trust board costs.[7] But the single most expensive reform - in adminstrative costs per patient treated - is probably GP fundholding.

GPs: whose side are they on?

Ours, we hope! We all rely on general practitioners. But 'GP fundholding' has created some odd incentives for GPs. What 'fundholding' means is that GPs hold a budget for buying care for their patients from hospitals, district nursing services, even in some cases ('total purchasing') from ambulance services and Accident and Emergency services. As pointed out above, this means that GPs are both 'purchasers' and 'providers'. Fundholders now care for around 60 per cent of us.

GPs have always been independent self-employed contractors to the NHS, so had to do a lot of paperwork. Fundholding, however, adds an expensive fund

---

4. OHE (see note 1), Audit Commission, *A price on their heads: measuring management costs in the NHS*, HMSO 1995.
5. *Financial Times*, 31.5.96.
6. *Guardian*, 7.12.94, and 22.5.96.
7. *Guardian*, 24.4.96.

manager. It also means that hospitals have to negotiate individual contracts for each type of service with each GP, and keep track of and charge for each GP's patients. This is far more expensive to administer than a 'block' contract with a health authority for a particular treatment for a large number of patients in one area. One estimate of these 'transactions costs' of fundholding is about £81,600 per practice, but as the authors say gloomily, there are no estimates available to allow comparison with health authority transactions costs.[8] The Audit Commission calculates that £232m has been provided so far for staff, computers and equipment for managing fundholding, as compared to £206m in 'efficiency savings' which can be retained by the GPs, and may be used for the benefit of patients.[9]

There is no satisfactory evidence on benefits to patients from fundholders' 'savings'. The Audit Commission found 60% of the savings spent so far had gone on premises (which GPs usually own) and equipment. Some have spent them on more patient care, including better levels of district nursing care, or extra clinics. There are some good incentives for GPs in these reforms.

'At least the reforms mean that you haven't got the constant haemorrhage of funds into hospitals. And we now have more influence over acute services. Previously, hospitals were fairly impervious to local needs.'

A GP (not a fundholder) in a deprived area, author interview

'The key benefit of fundholding is that for the first time we are being asked for our views on services.'

Fundholding GP, *Audit Commission* 1996, p19 (see note 8)

Both fundholding and non fundholding GPs report that they can now influence the services offered by local hospitals in ways which are beneficial to their patients. Fundholders contract with hospitals, and can threaten to go elsewhere. Many non-fundholding GPs in inner city areas collaborate with their health authority in local commissioning groups, and have a seen real change in the responsiveness of consultants to their patients' needs

---

8. J. Dixon and H. Glennerster, 'What do we know about fundholding in general practice?', *British Medical Journal*, 16.9.90.
9. Audit Commission, *What the Doctor Ordered*, HMSO, 1996.

The greater influence of GPs over hospital consultants appears to be the best new incentive to emerge from the reforms. However, a combination of the new GP contract and fundholding have also produced, or increased, perverse incentives for GPs. Both systems involve *capitation:* payments per patient. The weight of capitation in GP incomes has risen, and fundholding budgets are set on a capitation basis.

'Capitation fees are supposed to vary according to social circumstances, based on Jarman indicators of deprivation. But this is not enough to compensate for the much greater use of services in poor areas. My consultation time per patient is twice that of a GP in a richer area, and I have less time to do other things which bring in income. The census also greatly underestimates deprivation in some wards.' [10]

GP in a poor inner city area, author interview

If you have a fixed budget per patient, and commitments to pay for, or to provide, a given range of types of care, then the more you can exclude the expensive and demanding from your lists - the elderly, the severely mentally ill - then the easier your professional life, the better the service to the rest of your patients, and the greater your potential financial savings. Exclusion of this sort is called 'cream-skimming' or 'biased selection'.

There is no agreement about the extent of cream-skimming which is actually going on. Anecdotes abound about GPs refusing to accept patients onto lists, or rejecting unco-operative patients (those for example who refuse vaccinations, and hence reduce the income of GPs). There is also evidence of ethical rejection by GPs of such behaviour. But the *incentives* for cream skimming do appear to have risen. 'Cream-skimming in the specific context of fundholding is both technically feasible and financially attractive ... Practices with a disproportionate share of very ill patients will find themselves with resources well below the level allocated to other practices, whose population has a more favourable health profile.' [11] This is one route for greater inequality of treatment to be brought into the health service. And it reinforces the effects

---

10. Because of the influence of the Poll Tax on census completion in 1991.
11. M. Matsagannis and H. Glennerster, *The Journal of Health Economics*, 1994, p52

of the established bias in fundholding towards the better organised practices, which are disproportionately in the suburbs and shires.

It is also true that, despite GPs' close links to patients, not all their decisions on rationing care may be for the best. Doubts include the dangers of 'empire building': fundholders can benefit patients by bringing services closer to home; however they may prefer to be paid to provide services themselves, even if they would be provided more cheaply and of better quality in hospitals. This is the main incentive problem arising from the GPs' position as both providers and purchasers. Another doubt is the balance between very serious and less serious care.

'Fundholders determine the Community Psychiatric Nurse caseload ... In many practices therefore there is a move from on-going care for people with severe and persistent mental illness to counselling for minor mental health problems.'

M. Muijen and T. Hadley, 'The incentives war' *Health Services Journal*, 9.3.95

GPs, individually, come across certain kinds of severe and expensive illness only occasionally. Where they hold the budgets for it, therefore, they find it expensive when they do meet it. Meanwhile, they may tend to divert resources to more common - though still important - demands.

The point of having large health authorities was that they could spread risks and ensure that rarer acute conditions were properly catered for. They didn't necessarily achieve it, but there were no evident incentives against. This remains true of health authority purchasing. However, when purchasing passes to much smaller units, such as GP fundholders, the risk-spreading ceases to work so effectively and GPs may find it hard, or be unwilling, to pay for very expensive cases.

Ceasing to care

Once you divide up budgets into small amounts, used by different agencies for specific things, you risk boundary disputes. The worst one going on in the health service at the moment is over responsibility for the continuing care of people needing nursing and other forms of care because they can no longer care for themselves, especially the elderly infirm.

'A disabled patient who requires help with bathing is having to endure the indignity of having his top half washed by staff from Camden Council's social services depart ment and his lower half by district nurses.'

Hampstead and Highgate Gazette, 9.2.96

'One of the most worrying things about the NHS changes is what they have done to the attitudes of normal, decent professional people'

Christine Hancock, General Secretary, Royal College of Nursing (commenting on the above story), *Hampstead and Highgate Gazette*, 9.2.96

This humiliation could happen because since 1994 the NHS provides 'medical' care, and the local authority social services provide 'social' care. Neither is legally allowed to cross the boundary, both are strapped for cash, and no one can agree on which side of the boundary falls many a (much needed) bath. These boundary disputes cause pain to staff as well as users.

The Act which brought in the NHS reforms also provided for a huge change in the provision of residential and 'social' care for the elderly. It gave local authorities a fixed budget to pay for this care for needy local residents, whereas previously residential care had been paid for by the social security budget on a means tested basis, and there had been relatively little - but cheap or free - care offered at home by 'home helps'.

The background to the disputes over boundaries and responsibilities long predates the reforms: it lies in the rise in the amount of care needed by elderly people, as people live longer and can find less unpaid support. But the NHS has been withdrawing from 'continuing care' of the severely infirm elderly, and the social services have accused the NHS of 'cost shunting' by leaving the problems with them. The incentives here are certainly perverse: to waste time trying to push the costs into someone else's budget. But Christine Hancock's comment nails an even more serious and widespread worry: that in a context where people's primary motivation is about caring for patients, this kind of dispute induces cynicism and inappropriate behaviour. The net effect is deeply demoralising.

'Leeds Health Authority, in common with many other authorities, no longer has any long stay medical beds or contracted arrangements for such beds in private nursing homes.'

Health Service Journal, 10.3.94 (our emphasis)

This fact became news because the health service commissioner William Reid had just ruled that Leeds Health Authority had acted wrongly in ceasing to treat a stroke victim who could neither eat, move or talk, and had ordered the authority to pay the man's £330 a week nursing home costs.

Since the reforms NHS hospital trusts have been closing 'long stay' beds, and many now have none left. As a result of the case just quoted, the Department of Health issued 'Guidance' which, in the words of one commentator, formalises trusts' practice into policy.[12] The closure of long stay beds is not new, nor is the rise of private nursing homes. The number of beds in private and voluntary sector nursing homes, clinics and hospitals rose from 18,200 in 1983 to 145,500 in 1994,[13] while total NHS beds in England fell from 343,000 in 1983 to 220,000 in 1993-4 with half the decline happening before 1990.[14] It is hard to find figures on the drop in numbers of continuing care beds for the elderly, but Stephen Dorrell, the Health Secretary, stated that they had fallen from 55,000 in 1979 to 37,000 in 1996, at a time of rising demand.[15] Some observers think the decline has been sharper.

The reforms have not *created* the incentive to reduce continuing care of the elderly, but the financial pressures on trusts have reinforced it, the reforms have given the trusts powers to do it, and the community care aspect of the reforms have provided an opportunity. A current management catch phrase is that the NHS is about 'treatment not care'. 'Care' is increasingly means-tested, and paid for by families and patients.

If we consider therefore these two trends, the retreat from long term care of the infirm elderly and the rising management costs of the system, then in a clearly definable sense one has helped to finance the other. One cannot balance the costs and 'savings' directly one against the other: what has happened is that total real

---

12. D. Price, reporting on a study of the response to the HSG (95)8 circular on continuing care for older people, *Health Services Journal*, 28.3.96.
13. D. Price, see note 10.
14. CSO (Central Statistical Office), *Health and Social Services Statistics 1995*, HMSO 1996.
15. *Health Services Journal*, 16.5.96.

NHS spending has risen (slowly), so (less slowly) has demand for treatment and care, and so (sharply) have management costs. The retreat from 'care' has made some of the financial and political room for more administrative costs.

Perverse efficiencies

'OxDONS syndrome ... this department, which in 1989-90 could perhaps have been considered the ideal department - lean, efficient, good, even excellent, with no waiting list and superb staff morale ... had become by late 1994 unsafe, hyperefficient, with exhausted and demoralised staff.'

C.B.T Adams discussing the crisis in Oxford's department of neurosurgery, quoted in British Medical Journal, 9.12.95

The previous head of neurosurgery, who resigned over the crisis, attributes 'OxDONS syndrome' to pressure to base prices on costs, which drove the trust to use private patient income to subsidise price per NHS patient rather than to expand facilities. A reply by the NHS executive director of finance attributes the problem entirely to bad management of private profits by the trust.

At issue here is not the rights and wrongs of a particular dispute, but the widespread perception that hospitals too find some perverse incentives in NHS accounting rules. The problem exercising trust finance directors is that - like GPs - if a hospital starts out efficient, it is still expected to make the same rate of efficiency savings each year. There is therefore an incentive to 'pad' costs. Otherwise low costs can lead to 'financial meltdown' in the words of one surgeon.

'The surgeons claimed there was a perverse incentive to slip into financial crisis in order to secure extra resources.'

Health Services Journal, 23.5.96, reporting a British Medical Association (BMA) press conference.

'St James hospital trust, Leeds has agreed to operate a £5m deficit beyond the end of this financial year, despite NHS financial rules that trusts should break even. United Leeds Teaching Hospitals trust is also expecting a multi-million pound shortfall.'

Health Services Journal, 9.5.96

There is a double bind implicit in trying to 'manage markets' as a way of running a health service. The NHS rules involve setting prices based on costs to try to prevent trusts with local or regional monopolies from exercising power to push up prices. Associated with: a requirement to break even after paying charges on the capital passed to trusts when they were established; the relentless demand for specified unit cost/price reductions in each round; and (slowly) rising real wages in a labour-intensive service, this is driving hospitals into the red.

In principle this problem impacts first on the most efficient - with less scope for cuts, they start to get 'hyperefficient' - trying to cope with dangerously high 'throughput' - and quality drops. If they then see other hospitals being allowed to work with financial deficits, the incentive to pursue further efficiencies weakens still more. The incentive structures over the medium term reduce the search for efficiency they were supposed to promote.

Incentives and us

The problem with emphasising incentives is that we may become driven by them, and behave in ways we would not choose. The more people and institutions are paid according to 'performance indicators' the more they focus on getting those right. For example, the patients' charter focuses on waiting times, the government has emphasised waiting list targets, so the numbers waiting over two years for elective operations have been almost eliminated. Result: doctors charge that urgent cases are delayed to meet 'targets', and trusts are repeatedly accused of delaying putting patients *onto* waiting lists. So now data are being collected on waiting times for first consultation - we are chasing yet more data.

Information is useful - *and* it is expensive. Incentives are useful - *and* they are distorting. All health systems embody complex incentives - just like the rest of life. But the proponents of the NHS reforms cannot have it both ways. If incentives matter, then we have to get them close to right. We can't decide they don't matter after all just when they become problematic. The 'cream skimming' argument illustrates the point.

'The scheme's [fundholding] regulations offer little incentive to do it,
even should a practice GPs and fund
manager conspire to act against a

*'Readers inclined to reject our
analysis on the grounds that the
relevant lessons from the United
States are not applicable to Britain*

fundamental moral principle of general practice.'

The Audit Commission on 'cream-skimming' by GPs in *What the Doctor Ordered, op. cit.*

should be reminded that the ethics of medical care provision are partly shaped by the financial incentives in operation.'

Matsagannis and Glennerster *(op. cit.)* anticipating the tone of this objection.

Medical ethics are a powerful force, but one cannot appeal to them too freely while simultaneously urging attention to financial incentives. One is shaped by the other, and the greatest danger of perverse incentives is that they promote cynicism. The use of the word 'conspire' in the above quotation has an over-the-top feel: it suggests doubts in the writer. We don't need to conspire actively: a process of giving in, in perhaps small but mutually reinforcing ways, is enough to embed perverse incentives in behaviour.

There are no perfect cheap health systems that are wholly free of perverse incentives. The reforms have hugely increased the administrative costs of the NHS within a budget with a tight lid on it: the money has had to come from somewhere. By squeezing care in favour of administration , we appear to be rapidly worsening the financial crisis of a cash-strapped system. What we have done is institute an expensive form of competition for stringently restricted resources. It seems unlikely that the financial benefits accruing to patients in terms of better services have outweighed the costs, though we simply don't have the information to tell - and neither does the government.

Single-payer health care systems like the NHS - with finance channelled through general taxation or a single health fund - are the cheapest and among the most equitable in the world. Not perfect - but better than others. We are however putting impossible levels of strain on ours, both financially and ethically.

The notebook draws on published sources, and also the author's primary research in health and community care. Our thanks to our interviewees, and to John Clarke for comments on an earlier draft.

Cancer ward

Loretta Loach

A patient's view of the damage being done to our hospitals

Monstrous things have been going on in the health service: administrative scandals, financial mismanagement, and unnecessary human tragedy. Yet the damage being done to our healthcare system isn't only evidenced by the drama of these headline happenings. The inappropriateness of government action appears in the unrecognised experience of patients on a day to day basis too. These unexceptional but penetrating misfortunes do sometimes have a private cause. But more often they reveal what is injurious and harmful on a wider scale.

Three years ago I was given a diagnosis that was to turn my life upside down. Overnight I became a citizen of the National Health Service which was about to face a tumultuous adjustment of its own. It was a dank October day in 1992. Sir Bernard Tomlinson had just published his inquiry into healthcare provision in London. Apparently the capital was suffering from a surfeit of hospital beds, four thousand would have to go. A reasonable enough suggestion, all of us being against waste in the NHS (though how come only capitalists know the value of surplus?). So apart from the anxieties of my illness, I drew succour from the images conjured up by this report; I was about to inhabit a kingdom of plenty, being ill might not be such a dark experience after all.

Twenty four hours after Sir Bernard had become a household name among Londoners, I went into one of the hospitals he had targetted for possible closure: St. Thomas', overlooking the Houses of Parliament at Westminster. Because hospital is a place of confinement, the setting matters and St Thomas' commands some of the best views in London. The spectacle of the sun casting its brightness over the Thames is important to the sick who stay there, it's as if the landscape were an expression of our longing to be well again. Visitors are comforted by it too, the first awkward moments are often taken up with the pleasure of the view, a welcoming contrast to the picture of the hospital inside.

I had a rare form of cancer and I was being admitted for my first dose of cytoxic chemotherapy treatment. I waited for my hospital bed but some hours later, out of the fog of my fear, I heard an apologetic voice telling me there were no beds.

'The Government's overiding aim is to improve the health service for Londoners', Virginia Bottomley, the Secretary of State for Health, had said announcing the Tomlinson report. So things could only get better.

I was back again last summer for more treatment involving long periods in hospital. This time I got my bed. The fact that I couldn't have my treatment without it ensured me a place. The competition for beds though had not changed. I rarely saw one empty and if it was, it would not be for long, time enough to have the sheets changed for the next patient.

Competing for the single rooms on the ward was an unseemly affair. Private patients pay £275 a night for the luxury of a single room, more than the cost of deluxe accommodation in the Dorchester. NHS rooms bear no relation to these but they are coveted nonetheless. One of the wounds of illness is the loss of personal privacy. Some claims in this respect take obvious precedent: the room with an en suite bath was always occupied by a long stay patient whose cancer had so disfigured his face he wrapped the room around him like a veil.

The thing about hospital is that there is always someone more deserving than you. Most patients quietly classify their own needs in relation to someone else, real or imagined, who is needier. The health service benefits a great deal from this internal audit; like the deserving poor of the last century today's sick, who are mostly poor, spend a lot of their time being grateful.

Everything we read, hear and feel about hospitals tells us that they are places of scarcity, and no amount of claims about spending will convince us otherwise. So a pillow which I needed on my first stay in hospital was taken from a patient on a neighbouring ward, and the nurse whom I needed one night was taken by a patient who had died. The NHS depends upon the fact that demands made by the sick are minimal. We may want more, we may even feel we deserve more, but as soon as we cross the hospital threshold, we know we must have less.

One day while I was sitting waiting to see a doctor, an old man beside me began chatting about his bowels (the body has no boundaries when it has surrendered to illness). He was in a terrible state and he had been waiting over two hours for some medicine. Eventually I realised he was waiting for a laxative and that his wait was well beyond the hours he had been sitting there. Discreetly I told the nurse his problem and within minutes the man was smiling as she held out the yellow liquid on a spoon. It was acceptable to him to wait even though his endurance was needless.

The language of rights in the patients charter is hopelessly incompatible with the cash limits of the NHS. Sick people are more aware of their duties under the hospital regime, in much the same way as the staff. We morally identify with those who care for us as we each share in the suffering of scarcity. It's only because we are alive to the benefits of the NHS that we are horribly sensitive to its lack. But the walls of hospital wards are always covered in cards, a smooth blanket of appreciation for the nurses and doctors who work there.

'Most crying wrongs' said John Berger 'cry because there are no more victims to suffer them'. I worry that one day the best of the staff at St Thomas' will up and

> 'Walking into the day room the broken plastic seats and grimy windows finally got to me'

go to something better. At 8am when I was leaving the bathroom on the ward, I'd see the day nurses arriving for their twelve hour shift. One young woman I spoke to had decided to leave though she was halfway through her training. She'd had enough, and although she had nothing else to go to, she couldn't afford to continue, economically or emotionally.

I don't think any member of this government has ever gone into a hospital and seen what some nurses are capable of. In the midst of suffering and death they remain sensitive to the needs of others. One day I was watching a woman in bed opposite me. Her skin was yellow like dying wood and she was so weak she could hardly speak. It was a hot day outside and the woman was clearly struggling with the heat. A nurse on the ward came over to her; she lifted a drink to her mouth and then she began to gently brush the woman's hair. There was something very simple but moving about this gesture, and yet I saw other examples every day.

Hospital life is made up of feeling, in a way that government life can never be. I once felt such a burst of rage when, walking into the day room, the broken plastic seats and grimy windows finally got to me. I wanted to rub our eminent health secretary's face into the bedpan of the poor old lady next to me. I suspect that she will never experience the public health care system. I fear she will be taken care of privately; no hairs and filth in her sink, no snores or coughs or vomiting in her earshot, she'll hide away from the public she claims to serve.

On an exhausting occasion when the radiotherapy machine giving me treatment broke down and we waited four hours for it to be fixed, I joked to the nurses that I had been devising ways of murdering Mrs Bottomley. The most senior among them replied, happily: 'We'll provide the implements'.

In all my conversation with staff I never found one who spoke favourably of the Government. It's not that they have political affiliations elsewhere, they just seem bewildered by a government that can pay so much attention to the health service and yet be so indifferent to it at the same time.

It's bad enough for the sick when the hopes of healthcare are not fulfilled, but for doctors, serious doctors, it sharpens their sense of frustration. The Tomlinson report said that the capital had twice as many consultants per head than elsewhere. A consultant's productivity cannot be measured in terms of the number of patients he or she sees in a day. In fact, as any patient will testify, a consultant's efficiency improves in inverse proportion to the number of patients on their lists. A doctor can no more quantify his or her work than a nurse or any other professional whose job meets a need for care and help of the sick. It may be this fact alone which has forced consultants across a boundary; where once they were protected by scepticism and separated by their status in the hospital hierarchy, they now confirm themselves as part of the community in which they work.

Managers are the new outsiders in this community; oiling the wheels of a market reformed NHS brings them nothing but scorn. My consultant could barely conceal his contempt for them when, one morning at my bedside, he fumed that despite the doubling of their numbers, they still couldn't arrange for a sink to be unblocked. When I left the ward there was a line of scum and a notice saying 'not in use'. When I returned two weeks later, it was still there only this time full of filthy water.

Hospital life has never been perfect but this isn't the expectation of most patients. Surprisingly it is still the expectation of some staff; those for whom illness is more than a clinical entity - staff who are more attentive to the needs of patients than the patients are themselves. It is their gifts that the ill depend upon, treasures which have no place in the commercial lexicon of zealous marketeers.

Grey suits, no hearts:
Aliens in the health service

John Clarke

Something strange is stirring in the wards of British TV hospital dramas: TV images of managers in the NHS are contrasting their 'business culture' with the real business of caring for patients.

There are all sorts of reasons why health work makes for 'good TV' . The combination of life and death dramas with an ever changing cast of cases provides dramatic tension. This is often offset against the eroticised order of the hospital in which love and lust, dalliance and disappointment seem ever present possibilities. Small wonder that television companies on both sides of the Atlantic have found hospital life such a rich vein of entertainment provision. However, in contrast with their American counterparts, the British series have been striking for the way they have placed 'managers' as central elements of the dramatic scene. *Casualty*, *Cardiac Arrest* and *Health and Efficiency*, for example, have all made use of the tension between health professionals and para-professionals and hospital management. At one level, this may seem rather odd. After all, it is the US health system that is known to be the place of 'big business', straight-jacketed by financial problems and the province of endless innovations in 'health care management'. In American dramas, however, these issues tend to be part of the background context against which the dramas of medical interventions and personal relationships are played out. Unlike their British counterparts, they are not personified in ' managers' who are part of the day-to-day drama.

The creation of 'management' in the NHS was heralded as a progressive step - they could bring the necessary business-like disciplines to create an efficient and well organised health service. In particular, they were supposed to constrain the excesses of 'professional power' and make the health service more responsive to the interests of patients. TV series have picked up on the dramatic potential of the tension between managers and professionals, such that managers have become central features of images of hospital life. In Britain, management has become an essential feature of the drama. It is not that the doctors, nurses and ambulance staff have moved from centre stage. They still perform both as actors in the big life and death struggles of saving patients and as people bedevilled by complicated personal lives whose problems and pleasures are magnified by the closed world of the hospital. But their lives are further complicated by the presence of management - an alien force in the midst of health work. This presence of managers creates a new field of dramatic tension. The tension is essentially a simple one. The professionals (workers?) care. For all their personal flaws and foibles, they are, so to speak, patient centred. The heart of their work is about responding to human suffering and tragedy, and they suffer, too. By contrast, the managers are budget-centred, manipulating needs and costs to achieve the desired bottom line. Because of their ' business' orientation, they get in the way of responding to need - cutting costs, cutting corners and, in the last analysis, endangering patients.

In these dramas, managers are the carriers of 'business values' that sit uncomfortably with the provision of care. In *Health and Efficiency*, management was personified in Diana - a Thatcheresque figure obsessed by the problems of controlling the expenditure of the ' business' and referred to by doctors as 'Little Miss Money'. One typical exchange - with Sister Beth - concerned the cost of drugs:

> Diana: Since the last inventory General and Surgical B have used £42,000 of medication. I assume there's some sort of explanation for this.
> Beth: We are a hospital, Diana, we need them.
> Diana: Are we perfectly certain that our users' best interests are being served by giving them everything here... I mean, surely if they did without these it wouldn't hurt them?
> Beth: Yes, it would... They're painkillers.

Having discovered that placebos are the cheapest item in the medical cabinet, Diana then embarks on a campaign to offer patients the choice to 'upgrade' from their current medication to placebos - with a predictable lack of success. In such ways, being 'businesslike' is represented as an inappropriate disruption of the real business of looking after patients. The obsession with cost is directly counter-posed to the provision of care. But managers do not just embody this obsession with the financial 'bottom line' . They also represent a commitment to rational order which is portrayed as being at odds with the necessary and inevitable chaos of hospitals:

> Diana: We' re going to have to work out some system for this sort of thing [prescibing medications].
> Michael (Dr. Jimson): But people don't plan when to be sick, Diana.
> Diana: Well, they should *try*.

This is the stereotypical complaint of the manager. Their attempts to run things efficiently are constantly being subverted. Hospitals - and those who use and work in them - resist the effort to impose rationalised order on them. The will to power of these managers involves the wish to make things 'work properly' while the 'real life' of the hospital is represented as getting things done through chaos.[1] *Health and Efficiency* played this contrast between managerial rationality and the capacity of the medical staff to make chaos work for laughs. But elsewhere (though not *St. Elsewhere*) it is a deadly serious business. In the closing episodes of *Cardiac Arrest's* 1995 series a nose bleed led to the patient's death. A cost-cutting-induced lack of suitable medical expertise was at the root of the problem but a young doctor was set up to carry the can for hospital management. The antagonism between professionals and managers has also been a recurrent thread in the 1996 series, with the manager first conspiring with a homophobic parent to get a gay doctor dismissed, then blackmailing a student nurse to give evidence against another doctor - this time a rival for Sister Novac's affections.

Professionals are certainly flawed in these dramas. They may be arrogant (senior consultants), sanctimonious (bright young doctors) or frayed at the edges by too much pressure (practically everybody). But these flaws are usually redeemed by the fact that they do things for people. Managers, by contrast, are less ' hands on' .

---

1. J. Green, and D. Armstrong, 'Achieving Rational Management: bed management and the crisis in emergency admissions', *Sociological Review*, vol. 43 (4), 1995, pp743-764.

They provide no visible 'output' in the form of patient care. Their flaws tend to be the flaws intrinsic to being a manager - being pushy, ruthless, insensitive and crass. Nevertheless, they dominate the working environment in a distinctive and pervasive way. When *Cardiac Arrest's* Sister Julie Novac is summoned to appear before management after speaking to the press, she arrives in the suite of corporate offices with the following query:

> I've been asked to see the hospital manager. Now would that be the clinical director, the business manager, the administrator, the administrative assistant, the unit manager, the assistant general manager, the unit general manager, the executive or the chief executive, do you think?

On this battleground, health care workers fight the good fight - sometimes by seizing the high moral ground; sometimes by conniving or colluding over resources and sometimes by using cunning tactics that managers are simply not street-wise (or 'ward-wise') enough to combat. Human ingenuity triumphs - occasionally - over the grey suits. But the grey suits write the agenda - more throughput, less resources and a better bottom line. And there is something about the language in which this agenda is written that makes the grey suits perfect for the role of bad guys (and gals). Many of the dramas mentioned have caught perfectly the schizophrenia of a managerial language that is simultaneously both inspirational (the pursuit of quality; the creation of a customer-centred culture; empowering everyone in sight) and impoverished (driven by a narrow obsession with costs and control). Both the inspirational and the impoverished aspects provide the foundation for treating managers as detached from reality - or at least the reality of trying to provide health care. Celia Davies's recent research on health care has led her to identify:

> a form of 'gender talk' in the National Health Service that was unknown a decade ago. It refers disparagingly to the ' men in suits' , and questions the relevance of a ' grey suit' mentality that brings to bear an economic calculus that is devoid of human warmth and sympathy and that distances itself from the suffering that those in the frontline of health care must face on a daily basis.[2]

This also captures the imagery of management in the British TV dramas and

2. C. Davies, 'Competence versus Care? Gender and Caring Work Revisited', *Acta Sociologica*, vol. 38, 1995, p27.

sitcoms. Hospital environments are perfect for dramatising this imagery - those who care are physically marked by their uniforms: the white coats, blue dresses and so on. The 'suits' thus stand out - they lack the symbolic signs of being health workers. Hospitals thus permit the dramatisation of this difference much more strongly than other public services such as teaching or social work - or even in General Practice. The tensions around the 'mentality' may be as strong in other services but the signs are more ambiguous. As Davies suggests, this imagery is strongly gendered. As a result, it reserves a particular virulence for those women - like Diana in *Health and Efficiency* - who find themselves on the 'wrong side of the line' . Women-in-suits are doubly problematic. Women managers, however, are represented as having betrayed their ' nature' which should ought to align them with the 'human warmth and sympathy' of caring. In the dominant imagery of gender, it is regrettable but not particularly surprising that 'men in suits' should be associated with a managerial style that 'perceived as aggressive, harsh and confrontational' (Davies, p27).

These fictional imageries of management suggest that something has gone awry with the attempt to persuade us that what the health service needed was 'more and better management' . In this political scenario, it was the professionals who were the bad guys: arrogant, overbearing exploiters of their position as monopoly providers of services. By contrast, managers would discipline their excessive power, bring about efficiency and defend our interests as 'consumers'. TV dramas have inverted these images. The professionals remain the carriers of a public service 'ethos': they care. Managers, on the other hand, represent a different culture - one that threatens public service and the health of the nation. If TV representations are anything to go by, the cult of the manager-as-hero seems to have been a rather dismal failure. They remain alien intrusions into a culture of service and caring - carriers of a mentality, a style and a set of values that do not fit.

PHILOSOPHY

Radical

80 **Nov/Dec 1996** **£3.25**

Simon Bromley: Globalization Speak

Penelope Deutscher: Irigaray Anxiety

Michael Löwy: Walter Benjamin and Surrealism

Pauline Johnson: Nietzsche Reception Today

Peter Osborne on Honneth's *Struggle for Recognition*

David Archard on Bobbio's *Age of Rights*

Miri Rozmarin: Feminist Philosophy in Israel

79

Sept/Oct 1996

Jean Laplanche: Psychoanalysis as Anti-Hermeneutics

Mark Neocleous: Reading Schmitt Politically

Lawrence Venuti: Philosophy and Translation

Dylan Evans: Historicism and Lacanian Theory

Mandy Merck: Players at the BBC

Individual subscriptions
(6 issues)
UK: £18 Europe: £22   ROW: surface £24/$39 airmail £30/$51
(12 issues)
UK: £32   Europe: £40 ROW: surface £44/$72 airmail: £56/$95

Cheques payable to *Radical Philosophy Ltd.*

From: RP Subscriptions (S), Central Books
99 Wallis Road, London E9 5LN Tel: 0181 986 4854
e-mail: Mark@centbks.demon.co.uk

Public pensions and the private sector:

A new way forward

Jane Falkingham and Paul Johnson

The current public pension system in Britain is fundamentally flawed and requires radical reform. The authors propose a Unified Funded Pension System which combines fully funded pensions with public pension expenditure to support the life-time poor.

Pensions policy in Britain is in a mess. The basic state pension is now set at so low a level that pensioners with no other source of income automatically qualify for means-tested income support. The state earnings-related pension scheme is withering away in response both to substantial cuts in expected pension benefits and to financial incentives on offer to contributors who decide to 'contract-out'. Personal pensions have now been revealed as a very bad buy for many of the almost 6 million people who have signed up for them since 1988. Occupational pensions have weathered the storm of the Maxwell scandal, but tougher reserve requirements, to be introduced on the recommendation of the Pension Law Review Committee, will encourage employers to scale-down their commitment to defined-benefit pension schemes.

Each of these four primary types of pension has been tainted by the performance record of the last ten years, yet there is little sign that either the Conservative government or the Labour opposition has any coherent plan to restructure pension provision in Britain. In August 1995 Peter Lilley, Secretary of State for Social Security, said 'I am particularly pleased to note the steady growth since 1979 in the proportion of pensioners receiving pensions arising from their past employment, and from other sources, in addition to state benefits. The figures provide welcome evidence of the Government's success in encouraging people to make private provision for their retirement.' No mention here that much of this private provision in personal pensions has been shown to be inappropriate, nor that the scope for private provision by the low paid and non-employed is negligible.

Meanwhile the Labour Party, while strong on general rhetorical commitments to a fairer society and a new partnership between private and public sectors, has yet to come forward with any concrete proposals for the future of either public or private pensions, possibly because of the potential expense of any change in this most costly area of social security policy. In 1942 William Beveridge remarked that old age was 'the most important, and in some ways the most difficult, of all the problems of social security.' Little has changed over the last five decades to make the problem less difficult, but politicians seem to have become less willing to recognise any responsibility for delivering a reasonable degree of old age income security to everyone in society.

Think-tank 'solutions'

The vacuum created by the dearth of political action over pension provision has been partially filled by a number of private initiatives, most notably the (Labour inspired) Commission on Social Justice[1] and the Retirement Income Inquiry[2] (bankrolled by, but independent of, the National Association of Pension Funds - the trade association of the major occupational pension schemes). Despite their different origins, both these bodies identified two key problems with pension provision in Britain. The first, and most obvious, is that the ageing of the population

---

1. Commission on Social Justice, *Social Justice: Strategies for National Renewal*, The Report of the Commission on Social Justice, Vintage, London 1994.
2. Retirement Income Inquiry, *Pensions: 2000 and Beyond*, Vol. 1, The Report of the Retirement Income Inquiry, Chaired by Sir John Anson, London 1996.

will increase the demand for pension income in Britain, and this can be met only by increasing savings now (to boost private pension accumulation), or by increasing taxes in the future (for more extensive public pensions) or by some combination of the two. Given the reluctance of all political parties to countenance major increases in taxation, it seems inevitable that a growing share of pensioner income will be derived from private pension saving.

This leads directly to the second problem - that a substantial proportion of the population does not have an income high or regular enough to enable them to accumulate large private pensions. These people will continue to remain dependent on public pensions, but public pensions are already low, are declining in real terms, and are leading to a growing use of the means test to provide top-up income (already claimed by around a fifth of all pensioners).

'politicians seem to have become less willing to recognise any responsibility for delivering a reasonable degree of old age income security'

The responses to this dual problem by these two independent inquiries are remarkably similar. They both reject proposals from the TUC and the National Pensioners Convention that the level of the basic pension should be doubled in order to raise all pensioner incomes above the income support level. Not only would the net cost be enormous (£18.5 billion, or 9 pence on the employee National Insurance contribution rate), but less than a quarter of this extra expenditure would go to the poorest 2.7 million pensioners most affected by the means test, while more than a quarter would be distributed to the richest 1.8 million pensioners. Because the basic pension is a universal benefit it is incapable of being targeted on the poorest of pensioners, yet for reforms to be cost effective it is necessary to ensure that any additional tax-financed income is not provided for that minority of today's pensioners who receive substantial incomes from occupational pensions or other sources.

An 'Assured' Pension - old wine in new bottles?

The alternative advocated by both these committees of inquiry is some form of minimum income threshold (called an 'Assured Pension' by the Retirement Income Inquiry, and a 'Minimum Pension Guarantee' by the Commission on Social Justice). This would be provided for all pensioners but 'no means test (in the current sense) would be applied.' It is assumed that there would be no structural change to existing pension arrangements. The basic pension would continue to be indexed to prices, and so its value relative to average earnings would fall from around 15 per cent today to 9 per cent by 2030. Additional pensions - occupational, personal, or state earnings-related - would also continue unchanged. The innovation comes at the point of retirement. Each person's income from all pension sources (and possibly from other savings and earnings) would be totalled, and if it fell below the minimum pension level, she or he would receive a tax-financed supplement to reach this minimum. If pension income were well above this threshold, no supplement would be granted, but for those just above the threshold the supplement would be tapered so that each extra £ of pension income would result in the loss of less than £1 of supplement.

How does this differ from a traditional means test? It is argued that because the assessment of income is made at the point of retirement, and need not be repeated unless the real pension income of the pensioner changes in the future, it is administratively much simpler than the current income support system. Moreover, the proposed assessment is based solely on income, and all assets are disregarded.

We believe that this is semantic window-dressing, undertaken to disarm those people (primarily in the Labour Party) who are ideologically opposed to means-testing. In fact, we see means testing in some form as an *essential* part of a socially responsible welfare system; it is a highly effective way of ensuring that resources are redistributed from richer to poorer sections of society. The problem with means-testing in the past has been not the principle, but the practice - it has been administratively oppressive for claimants, expensive to operate, and has created poverty traps and other perverse incentives. Will the means-test associated with an assured pension be any different? We think not.

The idea of a 'one-off' income test at the point of retirement fails to recognise the fact that for a growing number of people retirement is a process of gradual withdrawal from full-time employment that may be spread over several years, rather than an abrupt transition. A gradual shift by an individual from full-time work to full-time retirement would necessitate repeated income tests until a stable pension income had been achieved. Even then an annual re-assessment would be needed to take account of the fact that not all pensions are fully indexed to changes in the cost of living.

Furthermore, the idea of restricting the means test to income alone will provide a strong incentive for people to accumulate non-income-generating assets (such as houses) rather than, for instance, making additional voluntary contributions to their pension scheme. Indeed, the prospect of an income test on retirement might significantly curtail the amount of additional pension saving currently undertaken by workers over the age of 50.

It seems that the 'Assured Pension' income test would embody the same fundamental problems as the current income support means test - inefficiency and unfairness. It would be inefficient because it would bias people's savings behaviour away from the patterns that ensure the best pension income. It would be unfair, because it would be assessing people at the point of retirement not just on their past financial capacity to save for old age, but also on their willingness to do so, and it would penalise the more prudent.

Pension assets at the point of retirement are a function of two things - the level of income received during working life, and the past propensity to save this income rather than spend it. An income test at the point of retirement cannot distinguish between these two factors, so would treat equally the high earner who lived an extravagant life and the low earner who saved furiously, if they entered retirement with the same level of savings. This is clearly unfair. To be equitable, the means test should be based on past *capacity* to save, rather than on past *willingness* to do so; in other words, it should be based on life-time earnings, rather than pension income at the point of retirement.

Ensuring adequate pensions fairly and efficiently - the UFPS

Is it possible to construct a means test for pensioners that is both efficient and fair? We think the answer is yes, but only if we are prepared to abandon the existing mix of public and private pension systems and think about radically different ways of arranging our retirement savings. We have devised a new pension system - we call it a Unified Funded Pension System or UFPS[3] - which is designed to:

* provide a guaranteed minimum pension for all people over 65;
* avoid all means-testing of people over retirement age;
* encourage additional saving for retirement.

3. The UFPS was first described in J. Falkingham and P. Johnson, 'A Unified Funded Pension Scheme (UFPS) for Britain', STICERD Welfare State Programme Discussion Paper WSP/90, London School of Economics, London 1993.

In addition the scheme would:

* combine public and private sector provision for old age income security in a unified scheme;
* treat men and women equally;
* allow fair division of pension entitlements between partners upon divorce or permanent separation.

The Unified Funded Pension Scheme is based on the principle that everyone pays a fixed percentage of their income into a personal retirement fund (PRF) which builds up over adult life and provides a lump sum on retirement. This lump sum is then used to provide a monthly pension income, for instance by buying an annuity. The contribution rate would be set so that someone on average male earnings would accumulate a PRF sufficient to produce a pension equal to half average male earnings.

'Personal Pensions provide inadequate pensions for people who have had low-paid or interrupted work histories'

This part of the scheme is similar to the existing system of personal pensions, although the gross inefficiencies of the personal pensions sector would be avoided by licensing only a small number of established financial institutions to receive these savings, which should ensure significant economies of scale. Everyone would build up savings in their own retirement fund which could not be plundered by fraudulent employers. Furthermore the value of the pension would be directly linked to this fund, and so could not be changed by the whim of government, as can now happen in the state pension system.

Personal pensions can be very successful for people with high and regular income but because the value of the pension is directly related to previous earnings they provide inadequate pensions for people who have had low-paid or interrupted work histories (for instance mothers, carers, the chronically sick and disabled, the frequently unemployed). In the UFPS, a person whose contributions are so low that their PRF falls below the level required to provide a minimum pension (we suggest a level of one third of average male earnings) will receive an annual capital top-up into their PRF in the form of a loan from the government, financed from general taxation.

Fairer Targeting - across the life-cycle
However, people with low income in one part of their life (such as a law student)

may go on to enjoy much higher income at other times (when a High Court judge), and it would be both inefficient and unfair to give them net capital transfers from the government. Therefore those who receive top-up loans during periods of low income would be required to repay this loan if their income and PRF contributions subsequently rise well above the average. On the other hand, if the person has low earnings throughout adult life then the outstanding loan to the PRF will be converted into an unconditional grant at age 65 so that a pension annuity can be purchased. All people will therefore retire with a personal retirement fund at least equal to the amount needed to provide a minimum pension (so no pensioner will have to face a means test in retirement), and those who have enjoyed average or above average earnings throughout their working life will have accumulated a fund sufficient to pay a pension well above this minimum.

How would this system avoid the inefficiency and inequity of a standard means test on income in retirement? The system of making loans to PRFs which are in deficit and of imposing automatic repayments when contributions are above the minimum necessary level prevents undue transfers to the life-time wealthy, but it does so without creating the labour-market and savings disincentives common to most systems of means-testing. All contributors pay the same percentage contribution into their PRF, so the means-test (more accurately, a claw-back mechanism) operates entirely within the PRF account, and does not affect take-home pay. This is equivalent to a *life-time* means-test.

In addition in order to ensure fair pension treatment between husbands and wives, we propose that UFPS contributions by both partners should be split equally. A non-working wife will therefore be credited with half the PRF contribution of her employed husband. Should this couple subsequently divorce, they will each carry forward half of their combined PRF contributions paid while married. Pension entitlements, therefore, accrue equally to married partners and are split equally on divorce.

This proposal for a UFPS shows that it is possible to devise a pension system which, despite being managed in the private sector and based on the personal accumulation of assets, nevertheless can provide a minimum pension for all citizens. It avoids any means-testing of people in retirement, it prevents tax transfers to those with high life-time incomes, and it guarantees equal treatment of women and men. Is this too good to be true?

The cost of running a UFPS would depend on both the contribution rate and the minimum pension level; the higher the former and the lower the latter, the less would be the cost to taxpayers of funding PRF capital top-ups. Our detailed estimates using a computer simulation model of lifetime earnings constructed by the Welfare State Programme at the LSE, indicate that, in the long run, a mature UFPS could provide minimum pensions at double the level of the current national insurance basic pension, but at marginally lower cost.[4] The key reason for this surprising outcome is that *all* the tax-financed capital top-ups would be targeted on the life-time poor - we estimate that 37 per cent of men and 49 per cent of women would need net capital top-ups (some at a very low level) if the minimum pension level were set at 33 per cent of average earnings.

The Costs of Transition - can we afford not to pay them?

There is, of course, a catch. New pension systems cannot be implemented overnight. They become mature only when all retirees have pension entitlements based on full contribution histories, and it takes well over half a century to reach this position. Transition costs - getting from where we are today to where we would like to be in the future - are the key issue in pension system reform, especially when the transition is from a pay-as-you-go to a funded system. The accumulated liabilities in the current national insurance pension system - that is pension promises we have made to ourselves in the past, in the hope or belief that future taxpayers will honour them - amount to well over £300 billion, and any transition to a UFPS would need to finance this cost, either actually or notionally.

We must recognise, however, that the pension system transition currently being effected by the Conservative government through the curtailment of SERPS and the gradual reduction in the relative value of the basic pension also involves enormous cost. Since 1979 the government has made enormous savings (currently £6.6 billion per annum) by indexing the basic pension to prices rather than earnings, yet this has occurred by sleight of hand. If this system of indexation continues over the next century, then the national insurance pension will have dwindled to almost nothing - and this must imply total transition costs roughly the same as

---

4. Details of the dynamic cohort simulation model, LIFEMOD, can be found in J. Falkingham and J. Hills (eds), *The Dynamic of Welfare: The Welfare State and the Life Cycle*, Harvester Wheatsheaf, Hemel Hempstead 1995, which examines the distribution of welfare benefits both between different individuals and across an individual's own lifetime.

those involved in a transition to a UFPS. The difference is that with a shift to a UFPS these costs are made explicit, and their incidence on different individuals and generations can be calculated and planned. With the current policy of gradual public pension attrition, pension transition cost are hidden, and are likely to bear capriciously on people according to when they were born, rather than according to their ability to pay.

I t is time for politicians to be more honest about the fundamental problems with the current pension structure in Britain, about the terminal condition of the basic state pension, and about the costs of changing to a new system. It is also time from them to be courageous - to reject marginal tinkering with a public pension system that cannot be made either efficient or fair. Our proposal for a Unified Funded Pension Scheme shows how a new pension system, based on the personal accumulation of assets managed in the private sector, can be combined with tax-financed support of the life-time poor, to produce much more effective targeting of public expenditure, and higher minimum pensions for everyone in retirement. Can the left ditch its emotional commitment to a national insurance system and a basic pension that can no longer perform at even a minimal level of adequacy? Can New Labour really 'think the unthinkable' and form an alliance with the major financial institutions to develop a radically different pension system for Britain in the 21st century? Over to you, Mr Blair.

 **DISCUSSION** Will Hutton, Charlie King
and Anne Simpson

Accountable insiders?

Reforming the pension funds

*The pension funds hold our collective savings.
Reforming them might improve our private
investment record as well as supporting us better in
old age. But can greater accountability be combined
with more effective investment?*

Pension funds are the conduit for the savings of a community, either a
community of workers in a company or a community of workers in a local
authority area, and the money is by and large channelled into shares on the
stock market. Their current collective value is in excess of five hundred billion
pounds. Pension funds own over a third of the UK stock market.

Anne Simpson, who is talking here, is an executive director of PIRC - Pensions
and Investment Research Consultants. PIRC are registered professional investment
advisors, but unusual ones. Their origins lie in a consortium of public sector pension
funds who got together in the 1980s to discuss how they could become more
responsible owners of company shares.

If you look only thirty years ago, around 1963, around a fifth of company shares
were owned by institutions, and the four fifths was almost entirely owned by

individuals. Capitalism in those days had real capitalists, individuals with money who owned shares. Now two thirds of shares are owned by institutional investors: pension funds and the insurance companies.

For Anne Simpson, these are *public* institutions: 'They're private in theory, but they're holding the public's money. When I say they are public institutions I mean they are intermediaries who ought to be accountable to those on whose behalf they invest. In that sense they have a public role, and there's a requirement for public accountability which is lacking at the moment.'

A lack of accountability

Early organising around accountability in the 1980s focused on ethics and employees' rights. Charlie King was a trustee on the British Gas pension fund for eleven years. At the same time he was a senior shop steward in the company.

I wanted to try and change the world a bit. I thought, it's our money so we ought to have some say in it. South Africa was an early issue when I was there. We agreed that we didn't invest in South Africa because it was a political risk. Not because we didn't like their politics. So that got everybody off the hook.

The 'hook' in question is the fiduciary duty of trustees, their duty to seek the best returns for the pension fund members. This duty can be interpreted to exclude ethical considerations from investment decisions, as Charlie King remembered.

Another issue was privatisation of water. I said, 'There are a number of issues about water: environmental issues, complying with European directives. I'm not sure water would be a good investment. And also, as a public sort of company and pension scheme, do we think it's right?' So we met with the other trustees, and they put forward the counter-arguments, and their last point was, 'OK Mr King, if you're not going to allow us to invest in water, you tell us where else we can invest to get the same return. And if you can't, then you're breaking your fiduciary duty.' That's the problem you're up against. You can't brush it off.

Anne Simpson argues that there is no conflict between good financial returns to fund pensioners' incomes and an ethical investment strategy.

Competitiveness is the foundation upon which responsibility is built. But these two dimensions are integral rather than in competition. A company over the long term, in our view, will not survive and thrive financially unless it understands that it's a social organisation with responsibilities. If companies over the last twenty or thirty years had been monitoring their environmental impact, controlling it, reducing emissions, many of them would not now be facing bills for cleaning up contaminated land. Companies like Shell and ICI are putting aside up to a billion pounds apiece to protect themselves against claims in the future. We can see an immediate financial consequence of an issue which five or ten years ago would have been considered an ethical rather than a corporate issue.

Can the pension funds, then, as owners of companies, play a role in a developing a more responsible capitalism? Will Hutton, the editor of the *Observer*, is also author of a best selling book, *The State We're In*. In the book, he refers to pension funds as 'absentee landlords'. He explains:

An absentee landlord is somebody who enjoys unearned rent from property: whilst they own it, they're not engaged with the management of it. It's power without responsibility, it's income without engagement, it's property rights without parallel obligations. And my sense of institutional share ownership in Britain in the 1990s is that it's much closer to that than is desirable.

The short-termism problem

The funds' disengagement, Will Hutton argues, cannot be justified:

Their savings, the dividends that they are enjoying, don't actually come out of clear blue air. They are the results of the endeavours of men and women in work places. These funds are owners of people's livelihoods. Now it may be extremely boring for this to be said, but there are obligations upon you to respect that, even whilst you're trying to maximise the money under your management, under your stewardship.

Anne Simpson identifies a 'curious irony'.

Britain is in the fortunate position of having capital markets dominated by long term investors. Who are - for a variety of historical and circumstantial reasons, and a lack of forward thinking and proper analysis - behaving like short term investors, not all of them but a large number of them...

The first responsibility for a pension fund is to make sure that it can fund its pensions when they fall due. That obviously gives pension funds a responsibility to ensure that the long term investment returns are matched with those liabilities. Simply in order to pay pensions in thirty years a trustee has got to be concerned about issues like capital investment in manufacturing, training, research and development and so forth.' Insurance companies too have long term liabilities...

During a recession, companies haven't made as much money as normal, but they are expected to continue paying out a steady stream of dividends to shareholders. If they cut their dividend or hold their dividend at last year's level, their shares will be marked down. Which is an obvious sign of failure but it also, then, makes the company vulnerable to a take-over bid.

What companies therefore do is pay out a proportion as dividends, salt some away to reserves, and when times get bad they raid their reserves, but the suspicion is that they also cut back on other budget heads to put shareholders first. Now unfortunately we do not have accounting standards which give a clear statement about things like research and development spending, advertising, training. But if they're cutting back on training their staff, on investment, capital expenditure, research and development, advertising, then what they're doing is sacrificing their long term prospects for their short term survival.

The companies in turn say 'Well the reason we're doing this is because our shareholders want us to.' So why do pension funds demand this? An immediate problem, says Charlie King, is the short time horizons over which pension fund managers are judged. 'The investment manager is measured every year. There are league tables, and if my manager was below the mean he was in trouble.'

And, Anne says, it's getting worse. 'Fund managers are increasingly paid performance-related salaries, which mean that their bonuses will be affected if they decide sometimes to take a long term view, and for example say no to a particular take-over bid.' PIRC aims to alter this pattern, by increasing the role of trustees in investment decisions.

I think that the chain of accountability from trustees through to companies is going to be an important part of having an investment strategy geared up to the needs of industry. It's not that we haven't got money to spend, but that we're probably spending it on the wrong things. As pension funds with liabilities over a thirty to forty year period, the sort of frothy returns on the stock market in the mid-eighties would mean nothing compared with funding capital growth over a thirty year period. So the issue is how to invest in companies that will grow over the long term. How do we provide a critical voice during the wave of take-overs and mergers, and as owners how do we support companies making an investment plan?

Creating long termism

Can this be done? Will Hutton sees the pension funds as just one part of the problem constituted by an interlocking network of British financial institutions which undermine long term growth and which need reform.

> I believe that take-over is too easy in Britain. There should be a public- interest defence for companies. I think competition law should be applied very aggressively, so that when certain thresholds of market share are passed, the take-over just fails. I think that some of the incentives for take-over, which are to do with the easy way that accounts can be bent, to demonstrate profits when in fact profits aren't too great, should be disallowed.

There are problems at the level of the firm too. Anne Simpson cites economist Paul Marsh. 'For him, the problem is that managers of companies don't consider that they ought to be looking for long term investment opportunities, or perhaps even consider that they don't exist.'

> Legislation is one key to change. Will Hutton argues for tax changes:
> I believe that, instead of giving pension funds tax exempt status completely, they should have to earn their tax exempt status through long-termist behaviour. The more they dispose shares in the near term, the higher the capital gains tax they pay, and the longer they hold equity then the lower the capital gains tax.

Anne Simpson worries about the incentives implied in such proposals, being wary about undermining the right to sell if necessary. In her view,

> reforms are needed on two sides. First, the Companies Act needs a complete overhaul. We need minimum standards governing the rules by which companies are run, model Articles of Association which govern the rights that shareholders have and how decisions are taken. We also need to look at the

duties of directors which currently are not codified in the Act. And we need to greatly enhance the level of disclosure because at the moment, for example, there's no requirement for a director to even disclose what his or her other directorships are, or past faults and failings.

The other side is reform of the role of the institutional shareholder. Pension funds would have a duty to exercise their voting rights in the interests of the beneficiaries. We also think that the rule which allows one third of trustees to be elected by the members isn't enough, it ought to be at least half. In the insurance industry, policy holders ought to be entitled to know what shares are held in the portfolio and what happens to voting.

Shareholder reform and company reform come together at events like the Annual General Meeting. Currently there's no duty on shareholders to disclose how they voted, and there's no duty on the company to say what votes they've received. Both sides are currently governed by Victorian thinking and the legislation clearly needs a complete overhaul.

Hutton would also constrain the optimistic valuations actuaries put upon pension funds.

I often laughingly say that the two bodies in Britain where there's an unambiguous case for nationalisation are the accountancy profession and the actuary profession. If we nationalised the actuaries, and made auditors responsible to the national audit commission, you'd get standard accounts and you'd get public interest valuations of pension funds' assets and performance, which put a lower value upon short term gains.

The aim, says Hutton, is a series of legislative changes which together sustain institutional reform.

Essentially what you're saying to British companies is, building corporate empires to inflate the ego of the Chairman, or the short term share price, is not actually congruent with the public interest. And we're going to build in a series of small measures which taken together really do hold the Leviathan down.

Developing active ownership
Many constraints affect active participation by trustees in companies' affairs. According to Charlie King: 'In the past we'd been absolutely passive. The only

time we ever met to discuss anything was when a problem occurred and it was usually too late then. One exception was the Pilkington take-over. We did have a special meeting over that and we agreed not to sell.' His pension fund developed policies on corporate governance, for example on political donations, 'but there was definitely one of the management trustees who thought that was none of our business, providing the company was being run properly and we had an adequate return.'

So strengthening pension funds' role in companies' investment policy involves major cultural change, and here collective organisation through PIRC helps.

We've been getting our pension funds clients to vote at Annual General Meetings. They vote according to a set of detailed critical guidelines which have been sent to the companies in advance, covering everything from receiving the report and accounts to accepting the dividend, the directors, the auditors. They raise issues like the making of corporate political donations, environmental policy; and as more funds begin to exercise their votes on an independent and informed basis so an important mechanism of corporate accountability is being put into place...

Last year we ran the campaign at British Gas [on executive pay] which put the whole issue of shareholder voting onto the front page of not just the *Financial Times* but of the tabloids. To have brought the issue of shareholder voting onto the front page of the *Sun* I think is pretty good. We aim to get this recognised as an important issue for the next century, and to give the public that sense of ownership; to instil in them the view that this money belongs to them and therefore they have the right to demand accountability from institutions.

Similarly last year we ran a director for the board of Yorkshire Water, Diana Scott, who got 20 per cent of the vote which is a very reasonable showing for a shareholder candidate, and certainly that put on the agenda what the deficiencies were with the Yorkshire Water board. And everything that's happened since then has shown that they need input from somebody with consumer interests and environmental concerns at the forefront of their mind. So I think a lot of shareholders would now look at Yorkshire Water and think yes we should have backed her.

Better company disclosure rules could strengthen the hand of trustees seeking to change company policy. 'Any government ought to be thinking about accounting standards, whether it's environmental liability, research and development or simply making sure that the financial information is transparent to outsiders'. Hutton wants to see more direct participation of funds in decision making: 'representatives of groups of pension funds should sit as non-executive directors on company boards, I think that's absolutely an imperative.' Pension funds as owners should, Anne Simpson argues, get involved in 'things like dividend policy, research and development, training, all sorts of issues relating to investment.' PIRC also wants pension fund money to support small and growing companies, seeing the lack of a thriving medium sized corporate sector as partly down to the lack of 'long term patient equity capital' which the funds could in principle supply - but don't.

Individualism and class divisions

Making this work, however, needs co-operation among institutions, which is hard to establish in the individualistic British financial system. Charlie King learned how difficult it was to collaborate with other pension fund trustees.

> It isn't easy. British Gas bought up a power station, and I wrote to every one of its pension fund trustees and said I would be willing to meet them. There were a number of common issues. But the message came back, 'you're twenty times the size they are and they don't want you interfering in their life.'

Charlie King thinks that a better way would be to have industry wide-type pension schemes with independent trustees. 'It would be a separate scheme altogether, not administered by companies like British Gas, and people who work in the industry could nominate the trustees and bring in advisors, so in some ways it would work like a trade union pension scheme.'

Will Hutton thinks that individualism and unwillingness to co-operate is deeply embedded in Britain, making us very bad at institutional reform.

> I think the big reason we're bad at it is that the institutions that we currently have do benefit a particular vested interest, hugely. So institutional change creates losers, who in the current institutional framework in Britain tend to be conservatives. It's very rare to find a Labour-voting member of a board of directors in Britain. It defines your middle-classness, almost, and your membership of the upper caste, that you vote Conservative. That's the first point.
> The second point is, this is validated by bad theory: a complete debauching of

a kind of nineteenth century liberalism, so that all outcomes in free societies are portrayed as the results of individual choice. Therefore people like me, who want to build institutions, are criticised as people who want to meddle with free decisions, who are going to construct a bureaucratic layer of government or quasi-government, and who also take away power and status from conservatives. You put those two things together, and, the opposition to change is fierce. That's why I argue for political change so ferociously, because I think that it's only the act of changing the House of Commons or the House of Lords or the judiciary, and demonstrating that creative thinking in this way is possible, that allows it to inform institution building in the private sector.

This theme of class division runs like a thread through all the stories. As a shop steward, Charlie King was first drawn in to pension fund affairs by efforts to get a decent pension scheme for manual employees, one which matched the staff scheme. 'A lot of companies still have staff-only schemes. So we started from that issue, and then I got more involved.'

He remembers the feel of the early meetings.

It's quite intimidating in a way. You sit round a big table, and there's us three at this end, and three from management who had the right of the chair. You then had several investment managers, in-house at British Gas. Then people servicing the committee, and somebody from the British Gas financial department, and a lawyer. Then we had two outsider advisers, and internal and external property advisers. So it's you on your own against all this lot, who knew the business inside out. After a bit of experience I knew what to look for. But that takes time. I frequently raised things that I knew would never go anywhere but it's worth raising them in front of the outside advisers, because they would go back and say, 'Yes there's a bit of a problem with this, you know.' Because it's all a matter of influence. If we had a problem we would sometimes have a trustees meeting, with our internal investment officer or the lawyers.

It is hard for employee trustees to develop the knowledge and confidence to cope. 'And they can soon wreck it for you. It's, 'Come on, this is a multi-million pound decision and I need an answer by three o'clock.' And you're trying to work on a building site at the same time, and talk on the phone.' Nevertheless British Gas was ahead of many other pension funds. 'The good thing about it was, it was a democratic structure. You elected people off the shop floor to sit there, and they sat there at the highest level. I could go out and ring up the pensions manager and say "Can I come in? I don't understand this? What is a bloody derivative?"

Trade union support, training and networking helped. 'The TUC and GMB do some really good courses, but it's trying to get the trustees in the frame of mind to know that they need it! Because the company's very supportive, and it's guiding you through, but it's guiding you through in their sort of way. So it can cut you off a bit from behind if you're not careful.'

Charlie echoes Anne's experience of the scale of the education - or persuasion - to be done. 'It comes back to why you're there in the first place. Do you actually want to change it? I used to do these couple of sides of A4 every year, saying what our policy was. I used to send it to loads of people. I think in eleven years I got about three questions. It was, "No, you're doing a good job, that's fine." "I know it interests you but it's really boring."'

Accountable insiders?

Because of the class-ridden nature of our society, a contradiction runs through the proposals for reform. All three interviewees emphasise the importance of democracy, openness and accountability but also believe that being an 'insider' is key to influencing change. They want pension funds to become effective insiders in company decision-making, and the British financial system to become more of an 'insider' system, where companies are more insulated from immediate shifts in stock market valuations by having long term committed investors.

But can you *have* accountable insiders in our class-divided society? Will Hutton agrees there is a problem.

> It's a dilemma. Two ways to go. You can make your pension funds insiders. Put members on the board. Not actually be very democratic. And become allies of capitalist Britain in a major investment programme. As committed owners the funds would give the stable platform from which this investment could be secured. You can go down that insider route. Or the other route you can go down is the democratic/ transparency route, which is PIRC's route. But you go down one, or you go down the other. What you're doing is trying to get engagement, and there are two routes to engagement.

Hutton's instincts are with the insider route. 'Well I have a problem with that, because I'm simultaneously, you know, a devotee of Tom Paine, and someone who recognises the power of insider networks in making capitalism work. It's a dilemma for me.' Hutton has drawn lessons from the German financial system. 'The German system is an insider system. I think I'm for an insider system where the lines of accountability are strong.'

It is hard to underestimate how difficult it will be to create such accountable insiders in Britain, where 'insider' is associated so strongly with secrecy and class privilege. Institutional reform needs both to bring far more people 'inside', and to open up decisions to public scrutiny. This partly requires reforming the pensions system itself.

Improving pensions means a mixture of compulsion, collective management of funds, better state support, and better investment strategy to provide better jobs and hence a more solid tax base. In Will Hutton's view, 'What you make compulsory is not the amount, but the fact of contributing. And for those people who are out of work or socially excluded, one of the things that their income support should entitle them to do is to pay a minimum amount into this personal pension which would become a kind of floor payment for everybody.'

These payments, he adds, could support a new kind of investment institution. You might contribute to a low-commission friendly society, established by the state with various stake-holders on the board. This friendly society would be a long term investing institution. It would be one of the sources for funds for a network of regional investment banks and regional development agencies. It would support the construction of a bank for medium sized and small business...

It itself would be a change agent, because the commissions and fees it charges would be so much lower that it would automatically be able to provide better guaranteed minimums than the private sector. And then it can do some creative things in how it invests. It would be a kind of Warren Buffet. It would be a combination of Warren Buffet and social citizen.

Warren Buffet is an American private investor, committed to long term investment and a legendary financial success. A 'combination of Warren Buffet and social citizen' is thus a really vivid image of an accountable insider. It's quite a challenge: to combine long term investor commitment with openness, and in the process to overcome the pathologies of what Charlie King calls 'the City club'.

 with Brigid Benson

Ethics in the investment market

Brigid Benson *talks to* Candy Stokes *about life as an ethical investment adviser.*

'In my twenties I thought, "Why should I worry about a pension or an income if I get ill? The state will provide". Now I know it won't.' This is the kind of story Brigid Benson, an independent ethical investment adviser who founded GAEIA (Global and Ethical Investment Advice) in 1993, listens to from clients every week.[1] Middle income people are becoming more financially vulnerable, increasingly under pressure to provide for their own pensions and welfare benefits. Flexible employment, which the major political parties seem to accept as inevitable, may suit some, but for many it brings insecurity, and can make regular contributions to pension and protection policies difficult to maintain, especially for the low paid. People moving in and out of employment, or juggling employment and self employment, struggle to plan for their future financial needs on erratic earnings.

This is where independent financial advisers come in. Brigid explains:

> People are becoming more financially astute, but we meet many who have no idea what unit trusts are or how pensions work. They come to us for an overview of their finances and suggestions about either saving regularly or

---

1. GAEIA is a member of the M & E Network Ltd, regulated by the Personal Investment Authority. The views expressed here are personal, and not the views of the M & E Network.

investing a lump sum. They want ideas - plans - that feel right for the next phase of their lives. The right level of security, some growth, maybe some accessibility, and a concern that they need this money in the future. People want to see their money grow, but they don't want it used to exploit or hurt others in the process. We can't always be certain that will be the case, but we can make sure some of the investments will be beneficial to others.

There is a growing demand for such ethical investment advice. Early ethical investment funds sought to avoid investments in the arms trade and in companies whose investments sustained politically dubious regimes. Now funds have more diverse criteria.

People are not just wanting to get a good return on their hard-earned money, but increasingly wanting to encourage good practice and caring companies - the sort they'd like their children to work for. Many clients recognise that they have neither the opportunity to go to shareholders meetings nor the time to carry out detailed research into company activities. They rely on the information which we gather from a variety of sources including organisations doing basic research, such as the Ethical Investment Research Service (EIRIS).

If people are to have access to ethical investment advice, some individuals have to take the risk of specialising in giving that advice. It's not the easiest way to make a living! Brigid began as an Independent Financial Adviser (IFA) in 1989, specialising in ethical investment. 'I started training and working as an IFA straight after working for a human rights organisation. I did not realise what a lonely, tough job it would be, or how different the work relations would be from the previous jobs I had done.' The challenge is to behave ethically towards clients, and to give advice on ethical investment, while running a private company in a generally unethical market.

Brigid had previously campaigned on third world development and environmental issues, as well as human rights, and her service appealed to many of her existing and former contacts:

Individuals, large and small organisations, and charities, come to us because they are convinced of the importance of ethical investment. We have never targeted affluent clients, believing that independent advice should be available to anyone, whatever their income and capital. However, it is generally the more educated and affluent that tend to seek out such advice. The less well off tend to get sold products by their bank, building society, mail shots, 'the bloke in the pub'. It used to be 'the man from the Pru' doing his weekly rounds, knocking on doors, that provided the only life cover that many such people had.

Inevitably, as independent advisers specialising in ethical and environmental funds, we tend to be approached by educated individuals, and by organisations with a strong social or moral stance. Our individual clients think and read and care about the world around them. There are many who have left highly paid jobs, or have been made redundant, and are trying to live a less materialistic life style. Many work in the formal public sector or in other sorts of public service such as the growing complementary health sector.

Clients visiting GAEIA fill out a questionnaire (in addition to the 'factfind' that all financial advisers complete with their clients) to indicate their areas of key concern. These may include nuclear power, repressive regimes, the tobacco industry, animal experimentation, and companies with anti-trade union bias. Positive criteria include companies involved with pollution control, energy conservation, production of recycling equipment, equal opportunities programmes, openness about activities, and a good safety record.

Brigid says many ethical investors want active fund managers, who use the financial clout given to them by the investor to raise issues with companies. Several of the ethical funds have performed as well or better than conventional investments. Advising about the most competitive rates of interest, as well as about ethical banks and building societies, is also part of the service. 'Clients are also informed about alternative, innovative investments which may benefit specific projects and communities. Those who have even a few hundred pounds of capital in excess of their foreseeable needs, can deposit it with organisations like Shared Interest and The Triodos Bank, who in turn lend to small business and co-operatives here as well as in the Third World.'

As a private firm which needs to make profits, establishing that the advisers will treat clients ethically is fraught with contradictions:

We earn about 10 per cent of our income from fees, and the rest from commissions. People are understandably wary that this will distort the advice we give. We try hard to recommend investments that are right for each client and organisation, regardless of the commission. However, few of our clients run commercial businesses. So they don't realise how expensive it is to employ people, have stationery printed, and pay the phone bills. We're not greedy - we earn less than most of our clients for working very long and sometimes anti-social hours.

I also enjoy helping to grow the concept of ethical investment, as well as representing our clients' concerns to the major insurance companies and financial institutions. We don't get paid anything for a lot of the work and servicing we do, and that means the apparently high commissions from a few clients have to subsidise these general services.

When I started I received some training and assistance from the conventional IFAs I worked for, but no clients or real professional support. So I decided I might as well set up on my own, and then join an IFA network. It was lonely at first working from home with only one very part time administrator, and no one to really share ideas with. IFAs, especially those focusing on ethical investment, consider themselves in competition with each other, so there is only superficial camaraderie when we meet. They are mostly men, and I'm not sure how many of them have been involved in the kinds of campaigns I still think are important. I don't think ethical investment offers all the solutions, it's only part of the picture.

It's less lonely now because I employ several people just to cope with the administration. We have about 500 clients, the number grows every week, so we are dealing now not only with enquires and new clients, but also the phone calls, letters and visits from some of the existing clients. A new adviser joined me in February this year because he liked the focus on ethical investment. (He's a vegetarian!) He was a senior compliance officer for a major insurance company, and is highly qualified.

Brigid is quite clear that ethical investment is only one contribution to better financial support over people's lives. There are large numbers of low income earners, and those in more insecure and sometimes dangerous jobs, who either can't afford or can't get the cover they need. And bad advice makes it worse: 'There are still some very poor value contracts around which leave people, particularly the low paid and ill informed, very vulnerable.' Moving jobs still undermines pension entitlements: they see people even in their 30s who may have had six or seven jobs, and have paid into a different pension scheme at each one.

Ethical investment enables people to express their concerns and values, and play a part in encouraging companies to adopt policies which lead to a more just as well as sustainable society. It is an important influence on the private sector; it is not a substitute for a welfare state.

Complexity, contradictions, creativity:

Transitions and the voluntary sector

Anne Showstack Sassoon

Voluntary organisations stitch together, often in contradictory ways, people, society and the state. Anne Showstack Sassoon *discusses the often innovatory nature of the voluntary sector in Britain and Hungary.*

In two countries with very different histories, Britain and Hungary, we have been living through an economic and social transition, but towards what is not clear. While ambivalence and anxiety are understandable, it is important to be in touch with what is being created as well as what is being lost. We are not living the death of the welfare state, but what we have, and will have, is something different.

In both the British and the Hungarian cases change is taking place under great

This article reflects on discussions between the author and Sue Conning, Vera Gáthy, Zsusza Széman and Colleen Williams.

pressure. The state sector is being squeezed, economic and social institutions restructured, and 'civil society' invoked. Yet no theoretical or political understanding of this transition is adequate unless it engages with the concrete. Indeed, a concept like 'civil society', which is ridden with contradictions and inevitably interwoven with the state, is only useful if it leads us to focus on key features of our transitions, such as the voluntary sector. The sector is crucial for people's survival and to the forms of outcomes.

Certainly, the voluntary sector, in either country, should not simply be celebrated. Yet what is also obvious from the experiences of experts and practitioners in the two countries is that however different the situations, state support and big bureaucracies of any kind only work because the voluntary sector, and especially women, stitch people into the bigger structures of society. This is often done in chaotic ways, as responses to pressures which can destroy what is valuable in a society, which appear messy, and are full of contradictions. Much, however, is creative, and it is this creativity which progressive politicians and policy-makers should facilitate, and political and social philosophers contemplate.

The term 'civil society' has had an important meaning in Central and Eastern Europe where the invasive party-state found any areas of autonomy highly threatening. In Western Europe, too, the term points to the poorly recognised role of social phenomena outside of the state. Yet criticisms of state bureaucracy and disempowerment, whether in Hungary or Britain, are not helped by an idealised view of civil society or community or family. None of these can be understood without considering what the state does or does not do and how public policy facilitates or hampers social creativity. Equally, the family and the voluntary or third sector provide the conditions for state policy to be effective, and ultimately for the economy to function.

Questions about power and voice, who articulates which needs, who is accountable to whom, fundamental to democracy, are sharply posed in this transition. In Britain we, too, are living a version of what the Hungarians call a systemic change. For the citizen in her daily life, the flows of information and lines of responsibility which run, for example, between local authority officials, voluntary organisations, joint planning mechanisms linking health and social services, local council social service committees, community health councils, with the addition of the various charters of user rights, and finally the electoral process, are enormously complex and often messy. These networks have wide implications for the very meaning of citizenship in Britain. Consequently, any idea of the British polity and the relationship between individual, society, and state which neglects the voluntary sector is woefully inadequate. The transition we are living through reveals the inadequacy of traditional categories and forces us to go beyond simple divisions between public and private, however defined.

Recognition of complexity

When Chris Smith spoke of going beyond leftist statism in his IPPR speech 'Social Justice in the Modern World' in May 1996, we find a political acknowledgement of the *de facto* significance of how welfare is sustained by voluntary sector activity as well as state guarantee. He argued that 'the principle must surely be that the state acts as the guarantor of all provision, the regulator of all provision, and the administrator of some'. He went on to say that '...it is time to get away from the sterile battle lines of public and private and instead to look at how the two can best work together in the interests of the citizen and in the interests of *all* citizens at that. In our modern world, I want a welfare system that works, that delivers social justice, that provides real protection...and I want Government to guarantee that to every citizen. How in every specific it is to be delivered is a matter for sensible judgment and practical analysis.'

Without supporting every detail of this approach, going beyond sterile debate is in fact only possible if we recognise that there is no simple dichotomy between public and private, that there never has been one, and that the welfare state has never, anywhere, from the Nordic countries to post-war Britain to central and eastern Europe, provided cradle to grave services.

This cannot just be explained by lack of resources or political commitment. It was because the family, in its multiple forms, and, in particular, women's caring work - and, in many countries where they were permitted, voluntary organisations - never withered away. They filled in the gaps and articulated and connected the needs of individuals, often under conditions of severe duress, with the services which existed. They patched together needs, resources, and institutions in highly complex and creative ways, which the Italian sociologist, Laura Balbo, has compared to the making of a patchwork quilt. Indeed, without these concrete intermediaries to connect individual and social provision, the state sector or large organisations in general could not function.[1]

For a worthwhile debate we need adequate language and apposite metaphors. Patchwork quilt or the weaving of a tapestry might provide a better sense of the complexity of providing for human needs. Sometimes planned, sometimes the result of spontaneous creativity, sometimes the outcome of shortages and chaotic, destructive pressures, made up of the old and the new and varying in style and shape according to different histories, cultures and tastes, the result may be a thing of beauty, or it may be a desperate effort to cover human need with the scraps available.

Certainly, complexity and the contradictions which this often implies can only be understood if we realise that the old boxes of market, public sector, civil society, state are not self-contained entities. Rather we might say that the different spheres or levels of society invade each other. Writing which refers rhetorically rather than concretely to civil society or to community, or to the family, and ignores women's and men's concrete roles within it and in society at large, or informal networks between friends, or the messy, highly differentiated, difficult-to-define voluntary sector, is simply inadequate however theoretically or journalistically polished. Engagement with the concrete will produce better theory and improved theory will help us to understand and to shape change.[2]

One way to make the abstract concrete is to construct a dialogue between an outsider, in this case me, with insiders, colleagues from Britain and Hungary who know the voluntary sector well. As the non-state sector develops in Hungary in conditions of democracy but severe economic pressure, the voluntary sector is becoming a significant part of the regeneration of a civil society and of the welfare state. And in Britain as we try to build something out of the devastation wrought by Conservative rule, no talk of stakeholding or of individual and social

---

1. See Laura Balbo, 'Crazy Quilts: rethinking the welfare state debate from a woman's point of view' , and Anne Showstack Sassoon, 'Introduction' and 'Women's new social role: contractions of the welfare state' in Anne Showstack Sassoon (ed) *Women and the State*, Routledge, London 1992.
2 I discuss the resistance to concrete analysis in the theoretical literature and its relegation to discussion about societies on the 'margins' and the lack of attention to the family and the voluntary sector in the literature in English in 'Family, Civil Society and State. The Actuality of Gramsci's Notion of "*Società Civile*", in *Dialektik*, Felix Meiner Verlag, no. 3, Hamburg 1995.

responsibility should ignore the social innovation already underway.

Responses to pressures to change

The British voluntary sector has never been completely separate from politics. Originating in private charity, legal changes in 1911 allowed the state to become its prime benefactor. In the post-war period, old and new voluntary organisations plugged gaps left uncovered by social services, put unrecognised needs on the public agenda, and constructed innovative relationships between members, users, decision-making structures, and services. The experience of working or being active or using services in the voluntary sector contributed to a critique of some of the limits of the post-1945 welfare state.

The diversity of the sector is immense. Groups range from large and medium size national organisations, some with long histories, to smaller, more recent groups, self-help and single issue, or tending to the generic needs of, for example, ethnic minority or gay communities. Campaigning and providing services, still relying to a degree on contributions and volunteers, some nonetheless so dependent on a state grant that its withdrawal would mean collapse, organisations became more and more professional in style.

From the 1970s, when local government grant expenditure was expanding, they provided an important voice for the excluded, although the grant-making process still meant that they had to gain the support of councillors and could therefore be considered an integral part of the political process. A dramatic change has come with the NHS and Community Care Act (1990), finally implemented in 1993, with a shift in the method of funding from grants to contracts, and in responsibility from health care to social care.

Few people who have not had some kind of close contact with voluntary organisations or the discussions around them understand how varied, complex, and distant from stereotypes of nineteenth century charity they are. Academic and political debates, which refer to civil society or community, tend to ignore the sector, other than to celebrate the pleasure and usefulness of volunteering. After all, all those women, many of them from ethnic minorities, often in professions which are highly skilled but badly paid, provide services and fill gaps, just as women always have (and of course they do not have to be women to do 'women's work').

These activities are so rarely recognised for the crucial social contribution that they are, except in so far as they cost or save money or help to dampen down potential social conflict. But if the abstract reasoning of the political philosophers manages to ignore one of the most important phenomena of the polity, there is no dearth of literature, academic or not, about the effects of recent changes in the delivery of welfare on the voluntary sector itself from the inside.

For example, the voluntary sector increasingly provides services once provided by the state. Whereas in Hungary the emerging voluntary sector is beginning to assert social needs, both Sue Conning and Colleen Williams emphasise that in Britain the voluntary sector's previous role of advocacy may be compromised, and the democratic forms of user participation eclipsed. The strain and indeed financial costs of having to respond to a changing climate of decreased state expenditure, of finding additional funds from different sources, of negotiating contracts for services which meet specifications, of monitoring quality and writing lengthy reports on process and outcomes are well documented.

However, amidst widespread fears about incorporation, new spaces have also opened up. Colleen Williams points out, for example, that the value to society of the voluntary sector is now easier to convey. Contract specifications require clear descriptions of what an organisation actually does. Without monitoring and reporting-back mechanisms, however onerous, much good work might never be recognised. She further suggests that being less dependent on the support of the elected members of a local council, as contracts are negotiated with council officers, may provide a greater opportunity for groups not traditionally favoured to play the game.

Who has a voice and how this is shifting is an important question to answer. Sue Conning stresses that small groups, indeed those very organisations whose existence has helped to put equal opportunities and user involvement on the political agenda, for example, lesbian and gay groups, or those from the black community, or with disabilities, may find it particularly hard to adapt to becoming more professional in the new contract culture without the managerial backup of the larger groups.

But small, local groups may be solicited to cover a need recognised by council officers, one which might not have been specified earlier, say, Asian elder care. Colleen Williams points out that some large and medium size organisations have had to trim their bureaucracies, and contract specifications may force them to think about user involvement and to take equal opportunities seriously for the first time.

Innovation is still important, but, as both Sue Conning and Colleen Williams suggest, directed increasingly towards providing services which not only are cost effective but fit into what contracts require rather than come from the grass roots, a very different picture from Hungary. In Britain, and in Hungary, professional and sectoral boundaries are blurring. Because in Britain charges are made for social provision, for example for elder care, the voluntary sector is *de facto* becoming the instrument of the process of privatisation, even though they are themselves not-for-profit organisations. On the other hand, Colleen Williams points out, they also can become the conduit for channelling state money to individuals, a process with parallels in Hungary. A contract can prevent misunderstandings through transparency, but, given the insecurity of competition,

> 'In Britain, and in Hungary, professional and sectorial boundaries are blurring'

it can also lead to lack of trust between voluntary organisations and local authorities. The suggestion being considered by Labour that contracts run for longer periods could therefore be a significant change for the better.

Not less state but different

Far from reducing the state, what we have is a directive state which has opened up some spaces for diverse responses but also calls most of the tunes. Yet if central government in Britain has undermined the functions of local government, the natural terrain of this discussion is still the local, since the application in practice of community care, with the largest effects on both services and sectors, is at the local and sub-national level. Indeed, in Hungary local government has an increased role as the central government withdraws. A common theme is the emergence of the voluntary sector as an expression of society's responses to change. In Hungary the voluntary sector, including mainly new but also some old organisations which have acquired a new role, is filling a vacuum and providing a different form of 'people power'.

The view from Hungary: the context

Abstract rhetoric about market, state, civil society is no more adequate to convey Hungarian reality than British. It is often not realised, for example, that employers in the past not only provided employment but also covered a variety of welfare functions. With economic dislocation and the newly competitive climate, these functions cease to be covered. Furthermore, low wages mean that households have depended not only on more than one full-time salary as in Britain but often on one or more people each having several jobs officially or unofficially. Further, very small pensions and lack of benefits cause old age pensioners to stay in the labour market, as Zsusza Széman's research documents.[3]

Consequently unemployment has especially devastating effects, bringing real hunger with it. State subsidies for housing, food, and energy have disappeared or declined substantially, and inflation has been high. Even state education entails charges, and everyone must pay for medicine. Many services, for example for the elderly, and types of benefits which would be taken for granted in Britain, simply do not exist at all. Family provision, especially across generations, has always been very important. There is a concentration of problems in certain parts of the country, particularly in the east where heavy industry has often collapsed, and agriculture is poorer than elsewhere, and amongst certain parts of the population, such as the Romany who may have large families and may have been re-located after the war, along with many people from the east, in new, mono-industrial towns that are particularly hard hit.

This situation is compounded by the central state providing a decreasing proportion of what is needed at the local level, with local government having to raise funds from an impoverished society. Overall, state expenditure has been cut back under the pressure of meeting payments on a huge international debt. Change is therefore happening in conditions of acute social stress.

This is the context into which new voluntary organisations have sprouted. They are innovating, building on the old, coping with the new, filling in the gaps often in a very unregulated way. Furthermore, the voluntary sector is a key player in bringing in outside money: an important channel through which aid reaches Hungary, which in turn is stimulating change in the social infrastructure.

As the old patchwork frays and sometimes falls apart, voluntary organisations are crucial to the survival of significant sectors of Hungarian society. They are pushing their way into welfare, doing everything from providing free meals and some home care, distributing donations from large or small firms of food, clothing, and even

3. Zsuzsa Széman, *Pensioners on the Labour Market. A Failure in Welfare*, Hungarian Academy of Sciences, Budapest 1989; and *Old and Hungry. Impoverishment of the Elderly in Hungary*, Hungarian Academy of Sciences, Budapest 1990.

energy saving bulbs, organising summer holidays for needy children and their families and social activities for elders, to mediating requests for help to large organisations.

The words of an Hungarian insider about two new voluntary organisations which developed since 1989, while specific and limited examples, not meant to represent the whole, can give a flavour of some recent responses to the new spaces and new constraints which reflect enormous ingenuity. They come from reflections by Vera Gáthy on research she and Zsuzsa Széman have done in the Third District of Budapest, which has experienced the collapse of heavy industry. They indicate new possibilities for creativity in a situation of

'Unemployment has especially devastating effects, bringing real hunger with it'

need unprecedented in recent history, in a context of the relative absence of legal regulation. They also illustrate the importance of pre-existing networks and of local government. Indeed Zsuzsa Széman is mapping the growing relationship between initially very suspicious local governments and the voluntary sector.

Civil society, social needs, and creativity in Hungary: two stories

Both organisations date from 1991, the period just after the systemic change when social concerns hardly appeared on the political agenda. The origins of the Association for Helping the Needy (RASE) has grown out of pensioners's clubs.[4] Vera Gáthy explains, 'They had a club room in what used to be the premises of the Communist Party organisation where they were allowed to stay. Alongside Red Cross clubs (also part of the previous, official organisations), they realised that there was a growing vacuum in social services. So thirteen people decided to set up an association and started to work on a highly flexible basis.'

Old and new skills allow them to 'react to new demands and to new possibilities. From the outset the chairman has been an experienced retired economist. He was very quick to learn about fundraising and has become a real expert at it.' Making use of the media, including a local cable television channel, 'he has been continuously on the move, going around to the 250 or so new entrepreneurs in the district, trying to persuade them to donate not only money

---

4. This draws on a taped interview integrated with information from a short written account and other conversations. Any distortions are mine.

but make donations in kind. They can offer the breakfast assistance because they get milk from a dairy.' Dinners and parties for the elderly are made possible, for example, because after an official function, 'a big company in the district which also has a restaurant' contributes 'the beautiful cold plates of meat and eggs which remain the next day.'

As it pushes its way onto the scene, the organisation is ecumenical about networking and sources of help. 'What they always emphasise,' Vera Gáthy stresses, 'is that they co-operate with everyone who is willing to co-operate'; for example, with the Maltese Charity Service, an important new national organisation which has Catholic links in Hungary and abroad.

Well rooted in the community, 'in close contact with the local health service and the local physicians, who give them addresses of those old people in need', nonetheless recognition by the local authority, run at first by liberals, required perseverance as well as common sense. Vera Gáthy explains that 'they were branded as communists. The local authority didn't even want to hear about these people. They tried to contact the mayor of the district who refused even to see them, but in the social services department, a reasonable woman who saw that she was unable to cope with the problems started to talk to them. They started to co-operate, and at least twice they even got small grants from the local government, and eventually got representation on the social services committee.' Co-ordinating with other voluntary organisations, 'mostly pensioners clubs or which represent old people's interests, or the Association of Big Families' was crucial. 'Altogether fourteen associations went to the mayor, and explained to him that "we want to help you," and finally in December 1994 they signed an agreement of cooperation. Now there is a dialogue between the top leadership in the local authority, and these organisations.'

The excitement of what has been accomplished is palpable, 'but it's also a political struggle. For instance, when they wanted to have a charity ball, and they invited leading personalities of the district and the country, it was only the two leftist parties who sent their delegates and no-one else.' The first national government after the systemic change, run by conservative and nationalist parties, 'had no social sensitivity. Neither did the liberal opposition. But now everyone has to realise that there is an enormous need for such voluntary organisations in the social field. While the leftist parties were in opposition, they obviously wanted to win over people, so they helped people out of both political considerations and social conviction. Now it is taken up across a wider political spectrum.'

Given a tendency in both Britain and Hungary to assume that the only substitute for the state is the 'market' , or vice versa, this is an enormous achievement. In Hungary it is particularly sweet because of the antagonism of the previous regime to allowing organisations any autonomy.

The other organisation, Pro-fitt, is an example of amazing social entrepreneurship centred on a dynamic, charismatic woman. It, too, organised a patchwork of provision linking expertise, other organisations and social needs, but with a different if somewhat overlapping set of networks. 'It was the initiative of a couple of people, in particular a Hungarian woman who was educated in the West. She learned a lot about foundations and associations and non-profit organisations, so by the time of the systemic change she felt that a voluntary organisation with very clear-cut purposes should be launched in Hungary as well.' The name, Pro-fitt, indicated, 'the need to improve the fitness and health of society since health care in Hungary, while it was still more or less intact, was deteriorating fast.' Making use of the Hungarian diaspora, sensitive to detail such as ensuring the supply of spare parts and servicing, 'Western hospitals, charitable and health organisations, and Hungarians living in the West' were asked to donate 'old medical equipment which was no longer being used in western hospitals but could still be used in Hungary' and equipment dismantled in Hungary passed on to neighbouring countries where ethnic Hungarians live. Support was obtained from central and local government, specifically the Ministry of Welfare and Health. The medical establishment also helped 'to specify what was really needed and how it could be integrated into the Hungarian network and to take part in distributing it. In a record time of two years there were hospitals which were practically re-equipped by her activities.'

Multifaceted, amongst its many activities Pro-fitt also provided services for refugees from the former Yugoslavia, distributing 'unsold goods donated by factories... Additional sponsors included a major Hungarian bank, a mixed, American-Hungarian company, and a Swiss one. It also kept in touch with a large number of non-profit organisations, including the Red Cross.'

But the ingenuity did not stop there. 'Management training,' Vera Gáthy explains, 'was offered to new voluntary organisations including a large number representing disabled people. She also knew that there should be some kind of co-ordination of voluntary organisations. She was instrumental in setting up a Chamber of Non-profit Organisations.' Perhaps the greatest innovation was to combine meeting the needs of the elderly and handicapped with environmental protection, more particularly glass recycling. 'In Hungary there was no recycling whatsoever. She found someone who had the equipment and technology, having decided that recycling should result in something useful.' Providing work for the disabled, 'the glass was ground and converted to scouring powder which, as well as refunds, was given to the old people who brought in the bottles.'

But the organisation did not survive the death of its founder. 'This is an example of how an organisation with very dynamic activities, with dynamic growth, with brilliant ideas, collapses once the moving spirit disappears because it had very little time to institutionalise itself.'

A few reflections from the outside

In both examples, with parallels in Britain, fundraising and advocacy roles are combined with providing help in kind and services as well as serving as the catalysts and conduits of various kinds of aid, stitching together social networks as well as resources, and making larger scale welfare financing effective.

In both Hungary and Britain voluntary organisations, from different points, are highly complex, gendered, sources of great innovation, and make welfare work. In different contexts many people in each country rely on them to survive, and society as a whole depends on the connecting threads that they provide which link needs to large bureaucracies and multifarious resources. They constitute part of the weave of civil society whose fabric is inevitably influenced by the state and politics. Politicians, policy makers, and philosophers should all acknowledge that the outcomes of the transitions in both countries will be shaped by this messy, creative sector of society.

These reflections derive from research funded by the British Council, the European Research Centre, Kingston University, and the Institute for Social Conflict Research, Hungarian Academy of Science. I take full responsibility for any mistakes, but I would especially like to thank Colleen Williams, for her intellectual and organisational contribution. It has been a pleasure to collaborate with Maureen Mackintosh on this piece.

Grants, contracts and NGO accountability in the north and south

Sarabajaya Kumar
and Ann Hudock

Sarabajaya Kumar and Ann Hudock look at the contentious issues of accountability that arise when NGOs contract to provide services

The accountability of 'voluntary' or non-governmental organisations has long been an issue of concern. Worries about how to sustain their flexibility and responsiveness to their own constituencies are further compounded by potentially conflicting demands for accountability to funding bodies. The huge rise in recent years of public funding of non-government organisations (NGOs) to provide social services in Britain has been paralleled by increased channelling of overseas aid through NGOs based in the 'South', for example African NGOs. Within Britain, but not in overseas aid, this funding has also changed form, from grant aid to contracts. Recent research challenges the conventional view that this grants-to-contracts shift necessarily reduces NGOs' responsiveness to users of their services, suggesting a more complex picture.

Accountability is best seen as a *relationship* where one is 'accountable for', and the other is 'accounted to'. This relationship can be between individuals, groups and or organisations, where one has a duty of accountability and the other has a right to receive the account. Grant funding systems have tended in the past to reinforce a narrow, one-way view of the relationship, emphasising conventional forms of fiscal accountability (being able to account for expenditure) and legal accountability (ensuring compliance with statutory provisions and regulations).

Organisations in receipt of a grant have to account 'for' what has been done 'to' the funders, who can apply sanctions, such as the withdrawal of funding, if the account is judged to be inadequate.

This notion of accountability has always been unsatisfactory, but the need for a new conception of the accountability relationship has been sharpened in Britain in the last decade by the shift in the role of government from 'provider' to 'purchaser' of services. Accountability to the general public has become more indirect and more complex. The public can hold NGOs to account for their use of public money only through government. NGOs must therefore enter some sort of dialogue with the government which mandates them. A new accountability relationship is required between the commissioners, deliverers and users of services.

The shift to NGO funding is justified by reference to presumed NGO characteristics such as flexibility, ability to innovate and proximity and responsiveness to users. If these characteristics are to be developed, so that services can meet users' requirements more realistically, accountability needs to be two-way and responsive. In other words, accountability should involve both the giving of an account and listening to what is said by funders, users and the providers themselves. Turning accountability into dialogue will not only inform decision-making but will also accord legitimacy to those decisions.

In reality, managing inter-sectoral accountability relationships can be problematic and messy. The government dilemma is how to ensure accountability for public money, while not at the same time undermining the responsiveness to users of the providers. The NGOs have to balance multiple, at times ambiguous and sometimes conflicting accountabilities to their various stakeholders. The fundamental issue for both sectors is how to achieve the right balance between independence and accountability.

The 'contract' is key in the reformulation and development of the accountability relationships between organisations operating in the public domain. This new form, initially seen as a pure attempt further to constrain NGO independence, has increasingly come to operate through dialogue. How contract accountability operates is now pivotal in ensuring NGOs accountability to the public (including government) and the users of services. Current rethinking adds to conventional fiscal and legal accountability, process and programme accountability: forms of accountability which are qualitative and subjective. Process accountability concentrates on how services are implemented and managed, while programme accountability focuses on the effectiveness of achieving intended objectives. While imperfect and an evolving form, contract accountability in Britain can encourage flexibility and participation, and allows considerable room for manoeuvre by both government and NGOs.

Contract accountability in Britain: room for manoeuvre

A continuing study of eight British NGOs providing health and welfare services through contractual agreements with local government has produced a strong and initially surprising conclusion.[1] Where there is a clash of interests among NGOs' stakeholders, and NGOs are balancing multiple accountabilities, contract accountability may actually operate to ensure that NGOs prioritise accountability to *users* over the demands of other stakeholders.

The research has shown that in Britain contract accountability, contrary to widely held perceptions of it as a constraining and rigid mechanism displacing NGO goals and diverting accountability away from users, in reality offers the space for dialogue. The research found that the negotiation process involved in setting up and managing the contract was invaluable to both parties, as it offered the opportunity and time for each to get to know the other. During these meetings, local government and NGOs put forward proposals, aired views, raised concerns about multiple accountability and response to users, and generally progressed ideas about the nature of the service to be implemented. Through dialogue and the development of ideas on both sides, a relationship of trust emerged. These discussions between the NGO manager(s) at the project level and local government manager(s) eventually evolved into a mutually agreed contract. This document served as a valuable reference point for those with a continuing involvement with the service.

The process of contracting thereby encouraged each organisation to increase the transparency of its own organisational priorities and goals. Both sectors had to be more explicit about their assumptions and expectations of their new relationship.

We illustrate the argument that a contract can ensure accountability to users with just one example: a critical incident from the British research. An NGO, which provided learning resources for young people and counselling for parents of

---

1. 'Accountabilities of large charities providing health and welfare services in the contracting state', research by Sarabajaya Kumar at Aston Business School. The support of the Joseph Rowntree Foundation is gratefully acknowledged.

children with special needs among other services, had its own management committee on which users were represented. It was funded partly by local government through a contractual agreement and partly from a variety of other sources, including regular and generous donations from the local business community within which it was located.

The NGO, inaccessible by public transport, also provided a meeting place for its users. By word of mouth, the reputation of the project spread, resulting in more people coming to attend support meetings, which lasted a couple of hours every few weeks. Attempts to make the meeting more accessible, including a mini-bus service, failed for a variety of reasons, and since the NGO lacked its own parking space to accommodate the newcomers, this led to problems. Nevertheless, there was plenty of parking space available in the neighbouring car parks which belonged to the businesses, and which the parents and co-ordinator had noticed were hardly ever used. As the businesses had supported the NGO through high profile donations publicised through local media campaigns, and it was common knowledge that the NGO was moving premises later in the year, the co-ordinator and users thought that the businesses would not mind if some of their car parking spaces were used for short visits.

They were mistaken. Some neighbours certainly did mind. A representative of one of them telephoned the co-ordinator's manager - the director - with whom he played tennis, to voice their objections. The conversation led the director to believe that if the parents were to continue to use the businesses' parking spaces, future donations might be withheld. Fearing the loss of substantial voluntary income, the director telephoned the co-ordinator at the project. He told her he would be writing to the users to inform them that in the event of any more complaints about their trespassing, he would have no choice but to withdraw the services.

The project co-ordinator vehemently protested. She asked the director to whom he thought the NGO should prioritise accountability: to some of the donors, who were his friends, or to the users, the reason for the NGO's existence? She also questioned the businesses' accountability to the users. She asked why, if they were so concerned, they did not confront the users themselves, or even threaten to clamp or tow their vehicles. The director informed her that the businesses felt uneasy about such a confrontation because in addition to recognising the difficulty about parking, the children also had disabilities and they did not wish to appear heartless. They were concerned, however, that their custom might be affected.

The co-ordinator proposed to ask the users for their suggestions at the management committee meeting, since she believed in user participation in decision making. She also reminded the director that should the organisation threaten to withdraw any services, then quite apart from jeopardising accountability to their users, they would be violating the terms and conditions of the contract with the local government commissioners. This would result in the loss of the current and any future statutory funding, and the relationship between the NGO and government would be ruined.

Concerned that her anxieties were not taken on board, the co-ordinator discussed the issue with the monitoring officer at the local authority, who in turn voiced her concerns to the NGO director and reminded him of the user accountability clause in the contract. The director subsequently telephoned the director of social services, who confirmed that the contract would be broken and indeed terminated if he threatened to withdraw any services from the users. In this case, the contract provided a mechanism for ensuring NGO responsiveness, and even strengthened accountability to users, by allowing local government to bring pressure to bear.

Grant accountability: cascading conditionalities

We now want to contrast this emerging dialogue-based accountability with the accountability relationships between 'northern' donors (governments and NGOs in industrialised countries) and 'southern' NGOs whom they fund to provide services in poor countries. This aid, in the form of financial, material or technical assistance, continues to be delivered by donors through the grant compliance system rather than the negotiated contract. Southern NGOs are the aid recipients; so they too face multiple accountabilities: to grassroots constituencies and to northern funders.

In the past ten years, northern aid donors have increasingly opted to fund southern NGOs rather than southern governments, believing them to be more responsive to grassroots beneficiaries, and more participatory in their approach to development. The process has obvious parallels with changes in service funding in Britain. The Organisation for Economic Co-operation and Development (OECD) estimated that official development aid flows to NGOs reached US$ 2.2

billion by 1992-93.[2] This scale of funding has brought similar demands to ensure that southern NGOs use the money appropriately.

T he chain of accountability between funders and service providers is however much longer and more problematic in these circumstances. Northern governments are likely to attach strict conditions to overseas grant finance, under political pressure themselves to account for the use of aid funds, and in circumstances where they find it hard to hold southern NGOs legally to account.

Research shows that these grant conditions may lead southern NGOs to alter their operations to meet these demands.[3] This may shift southern NGOs' accountability away from the beneficiaries and towards their donors. Some compromises jeopardise southern NGOs' integrity and the legitimacy of their operations.

The scenario becomes especially complex when northern governments distribute public funds to northern NGOs to be channelled to southern NGOs. Northern governments pass on stringent conditions to northern NGOs, who in turn pass them on to their southern counterparts. A further tier is added when southern NGOs pass the 'cascading conditionalities' on to their membership organisations. Case studies of local NGOs in Gambia and Sierra Leone in West Africa provide examples of the consequences of accountability without dialogue.[4] Southern NGOs are typically weaker than their northern counterparts, contending with problems which range from resource scarcity to difficulties in hiring, training and retaining staff. If their members' needs conflict with rigid grant conditions, this can damage their performance and effectiveness.

One example is the experience of the Gambia Rural Development Association. GARDA assists village-based women's groups with a variety of small-scale activities such as beekeeping and vegetable gardening. GARDA approached the Gambia Village Development Trust Fund, a joint Gambian Government - UNDP project, for a grant to set up a women's credit programme. The Trust Fund extended to

2. Data from Ann Hudock's study, 'Institutional interdependence: Northern NGOs' capacity-building support for Southern NGOs', at the Institute for Development Studies, Sussex; her forthcoming book is entitled *NGOs: Sustainable Idealism?* (Polity Press).
3. For example: J. Clark, *Democratizing Development: the Role of Voluntary Organisations*, Kumarian Press, West Hartford, Connecticut 1991; M. Edwards and D. Hulme, *Making a Difference: NGOs and Development in a Changing World*, Earthscan, London 1992.
4. See note 2.

GARDA capital at below market rates, but it stipulated the interest rate and repayment schedule which GARDA would have to impose on the borrowers.

The women found it hard to use the credit for small enterprise activities because disbursement coincided with the start of the rainy season - a time when they concentrated on farming - so they asked GARDA to alter the repayment schedule to meet their needs. GARDA could not do this because the Trust Fund refused to change the terms of the funding; the experience undermined the effectiveness of the lending and risked the credibility of the local NGO.

A second example comes from Sierra Leone. Five-years of civil unrest and rebel warfare has increased the importance of the local NGOs, as many northern NGOs have withdrawn or suspended their operations, and the newly elected government has scant resources and is institutionally fragile. One such local organisation, the Sierra Leone Adult Education Association (SLADEA) received a grant from a northern NGO to provide literacy training in rural areas. In light of the violence and insecurity outside Sierra Leone's capital city Freetown, SLADEA asked its donor if it could use the money instead to counsel displaced people in Freetown so as to lay the groundwork for future literacy work.

The northern NGO rejected the proposal, and advised SLADEA to hold on to the money until it was able to spend it on the agreed activities. The northern NGO justified this on the grounds that it had to account to *its* donors for the grants it made. Since the allocated money was for literacy training, it was concerned that it could not justify spending the money on counselling. The terms of SLADEA's funding constrained its ability to respond flexibly to the changing needs of its beneficiaries.

The irony here is that while donors choose to interact with southern NGOs because they perceive them to be responsive to their beneficiaries, the inflexibility of international grant accountability and the nature of the conditions actually undermine that responsiveness. The nature of the funding relationships between northern and southern organisations has at best skewed the development agenda of southern NGOs, and at worst eclipsed them.

Vast amounts of southern NGOs' time is spent answering the fiscal and legal accountability demands of northern donors. The problem is amplified when southern NGOs simultaneously rely on a number of northern NGOs for support, as the transactions costs in managing multiple demands become insupportable. If this is at the cost of responsiveness to the needs and priorities of their beneficiaries, then the NGOs will no longer be qualitatively different from the organisations they are supposed to improve upon.

Paradoxically, if the nature of NGO support and accountability does not change, increased financial support may actually hinder rather than help the southern NGOs. Donors argue that they must impose conditions to ensure the accountability and effectiveness of money spent, but the nature of those conditions and the way they are imposed differ strikingly from recent experience within Britain. Where NGOs funded to provide services in Britain have found that they could make space for dialogue and leverage, southern NGOs have failed to exert control over the conditions they face.

The continuance of grant-based accountability in international NGO funding may be as much effect as cause of this failure. The imbalance of power and the divergence of interests are far greater between northern donors and southern NGOs than they ever are between British NGOs and the government, and in extreme cases can lead to external control of the organisation. Southern NGOs are developing the capacity to influence their funding environment (GARDA found another funder who gave it more discretion) but they have yet to grasp the leverage they can potentially exert.

The scale and new form of funding of British NGOs to provide welfare services has generated spaces for some effective dialogue with funders. The contracting framework is being adapted by the increasingly influential service providers as a forum for negotiated conditions, assisted by movement of officers between the two (increasingly intertwined) sectors. These conditions can then sometimes sustain accountability to users when it comes under pressure.

But no such evolution is yet visible in the field of overseas aid. Relations between funders and southern NGOs are stuck in the top-down, grant-conditionality mode, with little mutual dialogue, to the detriment of highly vulnerable people and the local organisations set up to serve them. The coalition of interests and the strengthening of southern NGO leverage needed to change that - and to exploit the space offered by an incipient move to contract funding - are as yet not visible. Northern NGOs need to recognise shared interests in effective funding, and to shift the power relations in favour of their southern counterparts, through training, information-sharing, and support.

Stakeholder cooperatives in European welfare

Carlo Borzaga

The 'non-profit' or 'voluntary' sector is a key terrain for innovation in welfare systems. Across Europe, users and producers of welfare services are responding to deteriorating state provision by creating a new type of organisation. Carlo Borzaga describes these 'stakeholder cooperatives'.

All European governments in the last fifteen years have faced increasing financial and organisational difficulties in maintaining and developing their post-war welfare state systems to respond to changing needs. These difficulties have brought with them three kinds of very widespread reform. The funding and organising of many services have been decentralised to local authorities; while at the same time services have been restricted, and in many cases fewer needs met. Finally there has been a sharp increase in the number of private organisations producing welfare services. The European-wide increase in private supply of welfare services has turned the spotlight on the so-called 'non-profit sector', making it once again a focus of debate. The growth has been driven partly by explicit government policies of entrusting private organisations with the production of services which continue to be financed by the central or local state authorities: this has produced widespread experimentation with contracting-out and 'quasi-markets'. But private welfare has also been driven directly by consumers forced to turn to private organisations for the satisfaction of their needs which are no longer addressed by the European public welfare systems.

This process of privatisation of the supply of welfare services has not only hugely increased the number of private welfare organisations and the scale of their workforce; it has also modified their role and nature. Private non-profit or 'voluntary' organisations Europe-wide have moved away from the functions of advocacy, self-help, pioneering new services, and income redistribution from charitable resources, functions which are typical of contexts defined by well developed public welfare systems, and they have turned to being direct producers of social services. This transformation has caused, and is causing, a well-documented trend to professionalism and managerialism in these organisations. It is also producing a less well researched evolution of their organisational forms. The focus of this paper is on these latter changes, drawing on comparative European research.[1]

The organisational evolution

Organisational innovation among European private welfare providers appears to be producing a convergence on a new organisational form. Its most marked characteristic is membership, and involvement in management, by diverse stakeholders: users and workers, and also in many cases volunteers, benefactors and representatives of public bodies. These new organisations, which I call 'stakeholder cooperatives', operate in the welfare systems of almost all the European countries studied, including Britain, and have emerged mainly in the 1980s. Economic analysis offers some insights into why this has happened.

The economic literature has long identified a key problem with the private production of welfare services. Consumers of such services often find it hard to monitor the quality of the service they receive, and the relation of its quality to the price they pay. This allows a profit-seeking firm to reduce the quality of the service it supplies, and hence to cut costs, without altering the price. For this reason, market provision of welfare services is frequently unsatisfactory.

Economics furthermore suggests that one way to overcome some of these problems is to constrain the choices and behaviour of firms. These constraints can

---

1. This article draws on continuing research on the emergence of new forms of social enterprise in Europe, funded by the European Commission.

be imposed by a public administration, in drafting funding contracts with the private firms, or they can be voluntarily adopted by the enterprise. A very common voluntary constraint takes the form of a limitation on the profit-taking and profit-sharing behaviour of the firm, by creating a 'non-profit' organisation. Another is the involvement with the enterprise's management of the consumers themselves, or of stakeholders with interests close to those of the consumers, such as volunteers. In the first case, since the enterprise cannot distribute profits, it lacks an interest in increasing them. In the second case, the interests of the consumers are at least partly guaranteed by those who represent them on the board which takes the decisions on the quality of services. Across Europe, there have long been three types of organisation which exhibit one or both of those constraints:

* British non-profit organisations (mainly charities), characterised by a restriction on distributing profits to owners;
* 'associations', bound both by the pursuit of 'idealistic or social purposes' and by restrictions on distribution of profits;
* cooperative societies, mainly in countries such as Italy and Spain where cooperatives are recognised to have a 'social' character, with a consequent curbing of profit sharing.

The main distinction within these three organisational types is between the first two, which did not start out as producing organisations, and cooperative societies which have always been producers of goods and services. But these organisations are now converging, under the impact of increasing demands for private production of welfare as European welfare systems are transformed.

The big changes include a more widespread use of the cooperative form in the production of welfare services and, simultaneously, the modification of some of its characteristics. In the interests of consumer protection, attempts are being made to democratise the management, and to increase consumers' and volunteers' participation as cooperative members. Simultaneously, we are seeing a reinforcement of the productive character and activities of charities and associations throughout Europe. This has altered their organisational framework and brought the increased involvement, alongside volunteers and consumers, of paid workers and managers.

It is possible, therefore, to identify a general European tendency towards an organisational form that is a mixture of association and cooperative society. This new form takes in the strong orientation of associations towards the interest of the community (their 'idealistic' character), and also presupposes the participation of consumers and volunteers in their organisation and management. At the same time, it takes on the productive character, and the workers' involvement in the organisation and management of the enterprise, which are peculiar to cooperatives. This evolution is creating a new type of organisation, which some call 'multi-stakeholder'[2], and I have called 'multi-membership'.[3] For my purposes here I will refer to them by the more explanatory name of 'stakeholder cooperatives'.

Stakeholder cooperatives have the following characteristics. They produce various types of welfare service in a manner not unlike that of a profit-seeking firm, but their goal is explicitly neither profit, nor the economic benefit solely of their own members. Stakeholder cooperatives have a membership consisting of diverse stakeholders, especially users and workers, or workers and volunteers, or all three categories, but also including benefactors and representatives of public bodies. They aim for a democratic management process, which ensures participation by the stakeholders in decisions. And while they do not necessarily adopt a complete prohibition of profits distribution, they can usually distribute profits only to a limited extent.

Stakeholder cooperatives take on, according to the legal system of different countries, the legal form either of the association or of the cooperative. At least in two countries, however, this new form has been clothed in a new legal garment.

The legal changes

Organisational change puts pressure on existing legal frameworks, which evolve in response. The Italian social cooperative society represents an evolution of the traditional cooperative form. The founding Act of 1991 acknowledged a phenomenon that had been developed over the previous ten years. The main peculiarities of the social cooperative as compared to the traditional one are the following. The social cooperative must pursue an express social purpose. A legally acceptable objective however is to promote 'the general interest of the community

---

2. V.A. Pestoff, 'Renewing Public Services and Developing the Welfare Society through Multi-membership Cooperatives', *Journal of Rural Cooperation*, Vol.XXIII No.2, 1996.
3. C. Borzaga, 'Social cooperatives and work integration in Italy', forthcoming in *Annales de l'Economie Publique, Sociale et Cooperative*.

in the social integration of citizens'. The membership of a social cooperative can consist of a variety of stakeholders, including workers, volunteers, consumers and public institutions. And the social cooperative must be engaged in the production of social, health and educational services, or must employ disadvantaged people as at least 30 per cent of the total workers.

The social cooperative society may share out yearly profits only to a limited extent: not more than 80 per cent of the total profits and not more than the equivalent of 10-11 per cent of the subscribed capital may be distributed. If the cooperative is dissolved, members can be paid off only up to the extent of the subscribed capital, and any remaining assets must be put to use in the public interest.

'The social cooperative must be engaged in the production of social and educational services'

T he new Belgian form, the *'enterprise a finalité sociale'*, was established in April 1995 by an Act which modified the civil code. An enterprise can be designated a 'company with social objectives', if the company by-laws include the following: the social objective that the company is to pursue; a commitment that the members seek no personal profit, directly or indirectly; that the profit distributed to members be no higher than the maximum interest rate agreed by the National Cooperative Committee (at present, 7 per cent); that members' voting capacity be restricted to one tenth of the votes represented by the shares, or one twentieth of the votes when the workers also contribute to the capital; and finally that any member of the staff must become a member within two years of joining, except for those who do not enjoy full civil rights.

The activities of stakeholder cooperatives

Comparative analysis of the evolution of private organisations producing welfare services in Europe has shown that stakeholder cooperatives have developed in two main areas of activity.[4] They organise and provide social services, and more generally services of collective benefit to members, to communities, or to groups of citizens with particular needs. They also organise other production activities with the sole purpose of providing work, income and training for people with

4. C.G.M. (1995), *Social enterprise: a chance for Europe*, mimeo, Bruxelles. 6 P., Vidal I., (1994), *Delivering Welfare*, Centre d'Iniciatives de l'Economia Social, Barcelona.

employment difficulties.

Stakeholder cooperatives supplying social or collective services take a distinctly broad view of mutual aid, since their beneficiaries are often not members, and their membership includes people who gain no personal benefit from the activities and who offer their services voluntarily. They produce a huge variety of services, according to the concerns of the members, the needs of the community, and the nature of type of the public services available. Their services may range from strictly health and charitable services (such as care for the handicapped, the elderly, the non-self-sufficient, etc.) to those with a wider social scope (kindergartens, education), to cultural and recreational ones, and even to environmental services.

Comparative research has revealed great variety, and also some national oddities. The most common service production is for groups of particularly needy citizens on behalf of public administrations and with their financing. This is especially common in those countries where reform of the welfare systems has separated the financing (public) from the production (private) of services. However, a well-established track record of also producing services directly for private demand suggests that the current pattern of specialisation may not be definitive.

Stakeholder cooperatives producing social services for the public interest operate in many European countries. In some (France and Belgium) they mainly take the form of an association, although some cooperatives have been developed. In other countries (Spain, Portugal), where cooperative legislation is more recent, provision is made for the stakeholder cooperative form to perform only certain public interest activities, such as helping the disabled, and education. In still other countries, where cooperatives are employed to organise social services, the cooperative and associative forms used are the traditional ones, notably cooperatives for consumption, work, and production. But there is a clear trend to involving the workers or the consumers in the management of the company.[5]

In Italy, where the multi-stakeholder company has been fully recognised as social cooperative, it has been restricted to the production of only certain services. Conversely countries in which there has not been an expansion in cooperatives or French-type associations producing social services have developed other organisational forms with some of the characteristics of the stakeholder cooperative. Good examples are the community business and other small new organisations

---

5. Pestoff, *op. cit.*

providing social services in the UK, and the Social Solidarity Private Organisation (IPSS) in Portugal.

Another kind of stakeholder cooperative uses a range of production activities as a means of creating long or short term job opportunities for the disadvantaged. These have found it easiest to operate as associations or, more often, as cooperatives. In comparison to traditional cooperatives, and more like associations, these stakeholder cooperative place more emphasis on social objectives, restricting themselves to the task of creating work for their disadvantaged members. But the fact that, to meet these ends, they produce goods and services and must respond to the market, means they acquire a more entrepreneurial form. This type of organisation is even more likely to have a complex and multiple membership than those providing social services, since their beneficiaries are employed as workers, and hence it comes more naturally to admit them as members than consumers of services.

Comparative research has shown that this latter type of stakeholder cooperative operates in almost all the European countries, and that they developed mainly during the 1980s. Interestingly, they have grown quite independently of the pre-existing cooperative tradition or of other cooperative form operating in the sector of the social services. Their growth has been driven by the difficulty of integrating disabled workers into the labour market. The system of obligatory quotas and protected jobs in public and semi-public companies, common in European countries, worked satisfactorily during the 1950s and 1960s but failed in the 1970s. The growth of unemployment turned employment policies towards the new unemployed. There was less pressure on companies to take on disabled workers, and the protected work structures lost their original significance and risked becoming isolated ghettos, instead of helping the social reintegration of the disabled. In reaction, new production enterprises emerged, especially at the local level, which aimed to guarantee integration and stable jobs. By combining disabled and able-bodied workers, these organisations sought to achieve production levels that would ensure adequate remuneration for their workers and ward off the risk of isolation.

These initiatives then strengthened and spread in two main directions. Some organisations have substituted for the original intention of finding the disabled secure jobs in the company a temporary status aimed at rebuilding their working capacity and preparing them for new jobs in the open labour market. In addition, the target group has gradually expanded from the disabled to other workers with reintegration problems, such as ex-prisoners, and other socially marginalised people, including the long-term unemployed.

Thus the stakeholder cooperatives focusing on reintegration into work have steadily grown into an important instrument of employment policy mid-way between training and full-time work. They provide on-the-job training for people for whom standard training schemes would be impracticable, by employing them in work activities designed to provide training. This model of intervention is still largely experimental, sometimes created unreflectively, with scant formal structure for the training activities and for the passage between training and work.[6] However, it has a potential which employment ministries could consider more closely.

Research conducted to date on the various forms of stakeholder cooperative has mainly concentrated on more measurable aspects of their work. Qualitative analysis - especially of a comparative type - of the performances of these organisations is still rare. Some limited attempts have been made in Italian research on local samples of social cooperatives, and these have yielded some interesting results. Comparison between a sample of (single-stakeholder) worker cooperatives and of (multi-stakeholder) social cooperatives operating in the same sector (the maintenance of public facilities) in the municipality of Turin, shows that the latter have accumulated ten times more funded reserves than the former, and achieved almost double the rate of capitalisation, although the capital initially invested by the members was substantially lower.[7]

Another research study on 119 cooperatives working in the welfare services sector in Emilia Romagna concluded that those cooperatives which also have users and volunteers among their membership are less dependent on public financing, are more concerned to satisfy private demand, are more dynamic, and readier to develop new services, especially ones catering to needs not satisfied by other public or private suppliers.[8]

There is now sufficient research to confirm that the transformation of European

---

6. Borzaga, *op. cit.*
7. M. Marocchi, 'Le cooperative di servizi nella provincia di Torino', in Istituto Italiano di Studi Cooperativi 'L. Luzzati', *Il contributo delle nuove forme di cooperazione allo sviluppo dell'economia italiana. Il ruolo delle cooperative sociali*, Rome, mimeo 1995.
8. S. Stanzani, 'Effetti di reciprocità nel terzo settore. Dimensioni, aspetti operativi e criteri di efficacia della cooperazione sociale emiliano romagnola', mimeo 1995.

welfare systems has given birth to new organisational forms in the private production of welfare services. These forms are not simply characterised by a constraint on the distribution of profits - a constraint which hardly seems sufficient in any case to protect consumers - but they combine this non-profit form with the direct involvement in the enterprise's management of a majority of diverse stakeholders. The potential of these new organisations, and particularly the implications of their providing directly for the private demand of services, remains to be explored. This article is just a first step in identifying their existence, their increasing reach, and the extent to which they have already been adopted by the legal system of some European countries.

Jewish Socialist

NEW ISSUE – OUT NOW!

* **UNITED IN NO MAN'S LAND** Cynthia Cockburn on women's fight for peace in Israel-Palestine

* **EXODUS OF THE LEFT** Spike Katz and Muna Jawhary on why Labour   lost in Israel and the new scenario

* **WILLING EXECUTIONERS?** David Cesarani takes on Daniel Goldhagen

* **ALEXEI SAYLE** Mike Gerber asks him about comedy, politics and his Jewish roots

* **JEWS WITH ATTITUDE** Simon Lynn on how the community has surveyed itself and what it has discovered

* **POETRY** by Michael Rosen and Mordechai Vanunu

Plus – Asylum attack, growing old and radical, Cable Street, Israel's secret prisoners, short story, news and reviews
---**SUBSCRIBE TODAY**

I enclose £7.50 plus a donation of £......to subscribe to the next 4 issues of *Jewish Socialist*

Name...

Address..

....

Make cheques/POs payable to 'Jewish Socialist Publications' and return this form to *Jewish Socialist*, BM 3725, London WC1N 3XX.

Thinking collectively in the public domain

John Stewart

We need to reconstitute a public domain based on active citizenship, which would be an arena for public learning, for seeking responses to new problems. John Stewart explores some of the innovations in democratic practice that can strengthen that public domain.

The case for a public domain based on public learning is grounded in the government of uncertainty. The need for public learning has always been present, but has recently been highlighted by the transformations of our times. Economic, technological, social and environmental changes now pose problems imperfectly understood, which require us to search for a response.

In *Management for the Public Domain: Enabling the Learning Society*, Stewart Ranson and I argue that the polities of the post-war era neglected the need for public learning.[1] It was assumed too readily that government understood the problems faced and could deliver a solution through reliance on professional expertise. A system of government was built for certainty, which required no place for public learning and hence for an active citizenship.

In reaction, attempts were made to establish the neo-liberal polity, although never so successfully as its advocates sought. There was no concern for public learning, because the market would spontaneously produce responses to perceived needs. It is now realised that markets do not replace the need for public learning, but reveal it in the problems they create and in the issues they cannot resolve. The reality of the government of uncertainty has now replaced the apparent government of certainty or the assumption that the market will resolve public problems.

Reconstituting the public domain as an arena for public learning must involve the public as citizens, otherwise it merely reconstitutes the government of certainty in new forms. The argument for a public domain based on public learning is in effect an argument for strengthening the democratic base through active citizenship.

The Weakness in the Democratic Base

The British system of government is based on representative democracy, but on an attenuated conception of representation. It is as if the act of being elected constitutes the representative without the need for any further action, beyond making oneself available through surgeries to hear individual problems. This is a passive concept of being a representative, rather than an active process of representing or re-presenting the views of those represented.

The passive concept of representation leaves little or no place for participatory democracy or the active involvement of citizens in the process of government. There is a tendency therefore to see representative democracy and participatory democracy as opposed. Given an active process of representation, however, representative democracy requires and is strengthened by participatory democracy; and by participatory democracy more is meant than collecting the views of individual citizens. It involves informing, discussing and listening. Participatory democracy makes the role of the elected representative

---

1. Stewart Ranson, and John Stewart, *Management for the Public Domain: Enabling the Learning Society*, Macmillan, Basingstoke 1994.

more important.

The public do not and will not speak with one voice, but with many voices, making different demands. Within any area there are many communities, and lines of conflict as well as cooperation. The development of participatory democracy, if successful, should extend the range of voices beyond those normally heard. The importance of discussion in participatory democracy is to establish an awareness of different positions, to test them against other and wider concerns and to see whether, through discussion, new positions can be reached which can reconcile differences, or at least explore how far they can be reconciled. It is the role of the elected representative to aid that process, and in the end, if required, to balance and to judge differing views.

If there has been an attenuated conception of representative democracy, there has also been an attenuated conception of citizenship. In the welfare state, the role of citizen was that of elector, but beyond that little more than client. In the neo-liberal polity the Citizens' Charter as an expression of a market philosophy defines the citizen as customer, and in so doing limits the role of citizens or even their concerns. Even if I am not a customer of education, as a citizen I have views on education and a right to express them, as I have a duty to listen to others.

The attenuated state of democracy has led to and is constrained by a centralist culture. While many countries have come to appreciate that one cannot govern a complex and changing society in the certainty of centralism, centralisation has proceeded apace in Britain, weakening local government. Geographical and organisational distance separate central government and citizen.

Of course it will be said that citizens are apathetic. Examples will be quoted of attempts to involve citizens that have failed. The low turnout in local elections will be quoted in confirmation of that apathy. But too often attempts to involve citizens are on the organisation's terms. Little attempt is made to work with the grain of how people behave. Old tired forms of public meeting are hardly likely to generate public involvement. New approaches have to be developed based on an understanding of the reality of people's attitudes and behaviour.

Innovation in Democratic Practice

There is a need for innovation in democratic practice. While much has changed in policy and management, there has been little innovation in democratic practice.

For example, while concern has been widely expressed about local electoral turnout, there has been no attempt to improve it. Even the notice that announces the election remains as unreadable as it was when the design was first laid down many years ago. In New Zealand local authorities have the option to hold the election by post and now all authorities do so, because of the improvement in turnout. In Europe elections are held at the weekend. These are organisational changes, and do not necessarily deal with the real weaknesses of local democracy. They are indications, however, of the general lack of innovation in British democratic practice.

In two publications on innovation in democratic practice, I have set out a wide number of approaches that could be developed to enhance citizen participation.[2] Public bodies should recognise the need to develop citizen participation, and develop a repertoire of approaches to nurture the habit of citizenship.

The Informed Citizen

This article takes as its main illustration of the possibilities a family of approaches that are designed to find the informed views of a representative group of citizens. These are not the only approaches, and the range of possibilities will also be discussed.

There are three main defining characteristics of the approaches on which this article concentrates. They involve a group of citizens deliberately chosen as a representative sample of citizens generally, as the modern equivalent of the Athenian principle of selection by lot. In that way people from all sections of the population are involved, avoiding the danger that only the articulate and the joiners take part. They also ask from citizens not a continuing involvement, impossible to sustain, but a particular commitment over a limited period of time.

The approaches ensure that citizens only give their views after hearing about the issue in depth, with an opportunity to question and challenge. There is a fundamental difference between these approaches and opinion polls, which can be merely a device for obtaining the uninformed and often unconsidered views of

---

2. John Stewart, *Innovation in Democratic Practice*, Institute of Local Government Studies, 1995; John Stewart, *Further Innovation in Democratic Practice*, Institute of Local Government Studies, 1996.

citizens. Recently the Local Government Commission for England sought citizens' views on local government reorganisation in most counties. Generally they showed opinions were divided, although there was a tendency to favour 'no change' in many areas. However, on one issue there was general agreement; about 80 per cent on average said they knew nothing or very little about the issues on which they were giving their view. One might consider that that robbed their views of some of their value.

These approaches also ensure that the citizens involved have discussed the issues amongst themselves. Democracy, if it is to be meaningful, must be more than a recording system for individual views. It should involve discourse in which citizens explore views together, test ideas, seek agreement, yet become aware of difference. These approaches bring deliberation by citizens into the process of government. As Fishkin has argued:

> The distinction between the inclinations of the moment and public opinions that are refined by 'sedate reflection' is an essential part of any adequate theory of democracy. Political equality without deliberation is not of much use, for it amounts to nothing more than the power without the opportunity to think about how that power could be exercised.[3]

Although the numbers involved are small they are a microcosm of the citizenry at large.

Citizens' Juries

Citizens' juries are an example of these approaches. Citizens' juries were developed independently in Germany, where are they called planning cells, and in the United States. A group of citizens representing the general public meet together to explore a policy issue or to discuss a particular decision. Witnesses present information and jurors ask questions. They then deliberate amongst themselves before making their conclusions public.

Normally in Germany and the United States citizens' juries last about four to five days. In that time, it has been found that citizens develop a good understanding of the issues involved, and effective discussion develops. Jurors find it a rewarding

---

3. James Fishkin, *Democracy and Deliberation: New Directions for Democratic Reform*, Yale University Press, 1991.

experience and can become advocates for its further development.

Citizens' juries are not used as decision-making bodies. They are a source of advice and guidance for decision-makers on issues on which they seek to learn the views of informed citizens. Normally the decision-maker will easily learn the views of interested parties, at least if they belong to groups having ease of access to government. They can learn through opinion polls the, too often, uninformed views of citizens. They do not readily have access to the informed views of citizens.

There are issues on which elected representatives are uncertain how to proceed. They may be unconvinced by the professional advice they receive, but be uncertain of the public's attitude. They may be aware of conflicts of views between interested parties or the pressure of particular parties, and will wish to know what the views of the public generally would be if informed about the issue. In fields of policy where new issues are arising they may seek ideas from an informed public.

In all these circumstances and others, decision-makers may seek the views of a citizens' jury. In Germany where the use of citizens' juries is more developed, Professor Peter Dienel and the Research Institute for Public Participation and Planning Procedures at the University of Wuppertal accept commissions from local authorities, the Länder and federal government. The authority commissioning the citizens' jury does not undertake to accept its views. It will however undertake to consider the views expressed and to respond to them. This emphasises that the role of the citizens' juries is not decision-making, but to inform decision-making, in the same way as participatory democracy generally has been presented as informing, not replacing, representative democracy.

Citizens' juries were used to consider designs for development in and around Cologne City Square, and led to reconsideration of the proposals of the council's professional advisers. One wonders whether some town centre developments in Britain would have survived appraisal by citizens' juries. In Grevelsburg a citizens' jury examined alternative approaches to traffic problems in a historic town centre. Citizens' juries have also been used to explore broader policy issues on which they may well produce guidelines rather than specific recommendations. In Germany they have considered the social consequences of new technology and in Greater New Haven in the United States they have explored the problems of at-risk children.

The phrase 'citizens' juries' commands attention and connects the development with an established tradition involving citizens in the process of government. It can mislead however, because the process differs from the formality of courts of law - and indeed the phrase is not used in Germany. There is no judge, but rather a moderator whose role is to facilitate discussion and certainly not to maintain quasi-legal procedures. The jury does not have to reach agreement, but only record its different views if agreement is not reached. Importance is attached to discussion which can take place throughout the process. In Germany, with juries of 25, some of the discussion takes place in groups of five, before coming back to the wider group. The emphasis is on informality in easing discussion.

One of the main problems with citizens' juries is to avoid bias and ensure the integrity of the process. In Germany and America (at the Jefferson Centre in Minneapolis, where Ned Crosby originated the phrase) this is the responsibility of the independent centres who organise the citizens' juries, and whose reputation depends upon the integrity of the process. While the sponsoring organisation will specify the issue to be the subject of the jury, the charge (or way the issue is posed) will be determined by the organisers. They will control the selection of the jury and seek to secure it is a representative group. The organisers will also select the witnesses and control the information provided.

Citizens' juries naturally involve costs, particularly since some form of payment is made to jurors. Costs can vary from £10,000 up to over £100,000, when multiple juries are involved. Equivalent costs may be involved in other means of investigating issues, including of course opinion surveys. Citizens' juries should be seen as one means of investigating public issues through the exercise of citizenship.

Since the publication of the Institute of Public Policy Research's work on Citizens' Juries there has been considerable interest in their potential in local authorities.[4] The Local Government Management Board has sponsored a series of pilot projects. Over forty authorities expressed interest in the projects and six were chosen to proceed. The issues covered include the impact of new technology, drugs issues and the improvement of a specific area of a town.

There has also been interest in health authorities. This is seen as, in part, a

---

4. John Stewart, Liz Kendall and Anna Coote , *Citizens' Juries*, Institute of Public Policy Research, London 1994.

means of enhancing their own accountability, as concern with the accountability of appointed boards has grown. The Institute of Public Policy Research and the King's Fund are supporting a number of citizens' juries in health authorities focusing on such issues as health rationing.

These citizens' juries in this country are being undertaken as this article is being written. There will be evaluations of their success and their impact on authorities. For the purpose of this article they have been used as an example of innovation in democratic practice. Citizen involvement can take different forms. Citizens' juries are not *the* approach to building participatory democracy, but *an* approach amongst a repertoire of approaches designed to find the informed views of citizens. Here, more briefly, are several others.

Deliberative Opinion Polls

Deliberative opinion polls also seek the informed views of citizens. However, while citizens' juries take as their starting point the jury system and then modify it, the deliberative opinion poll takes as its starting point the opinion poll and seeks to overcome its weakness. Fishkin, its main advocate, has argued, 'An ordinary opinion poll models what the public thinks, given how little it knows. A deliberative opinion poll models what the public would think, if it had a more adequate chance to think about the questions at issue.'[5]

Deliberative opinion polls differ from citizens' juries in that they involve larger numbers and can involve less time and less intense discussion. They differ from normal opinion polls in that opinions will be tested after the participants have had an opportunity to hear witnesses, ask questions and discuss the issue, although for the purpose of comparison views may also have been tested at the outset of the process.

Fishkin piloted a deliberative opinion poll on issues of law and order in Britain through Channel Four television and the *Independent* newspaper. In January of this year a National Issues convention was held in the United States which included a deliberative opinion poll based on six hundred voters selected as a representative sample of the American population. They discussed key issues facing America, including the economy, America's role in the world and the state of the family.

---

5. Fishkin, *op. cit.*

Citizens' Panels

Citizens' panels are representative panels of citizens called together as sounding boards. In 1993 eight health panels, each consisting of twelve people selected to be a representative sample of the population, were set up by the Somerset Health Commission to discuss the values that should guide health resource allocation decisions. The panels held four meetings over the following year. At the first meeting panel members were asked to bring their own health issues. At the succeeding meeting they discussed issues raised by the health authorities. These included whether the health authority should pay for coronary artery by-pass operations for people who smoke, and whether certain treatments should be given at all. The topics chosen were issues being actively considered by the authorities.

There is an emphasis on deliberation: 'An important rationale of our approach to consultation was that those involved should have the opportunity to explore issues in some depth. Most people need a period of listening to the views of others and talking about issues themselves in order to clarify their thoughts on any complex questions.'[6] After discussion, panel members complete a series of decision sheets, in effect voting on the issue. The research team organising the project prepared reports for the health authority on the panels, using the discussion to convey the flavour of the panel meeting as well as the results from the decision sheets. The panels are continuing with four members of the panels replaced at each meeting.

The same principle has been suggested for a local authority, but with a panel of 200 to 300, to meet once a month, as a sounding board for the authority, again with a number changing each month. The panel would again be a representative panel ensuring that sections of the public were represented from whom the authority rarely heard views.

Consensus Conferences

Consensus conferences are another variant. They were designed to incorporate public interests and concerns into processes of science policy-making, which has often been seen as a matter for experts but increasingly raises ethical or environmental issues. This approach was developed in Denmark and a consensus conference was organised in Britain by the Science Museum in London on plant biotechnology.

---

6. Anne Richardson and Wendy Sykes, *Eliciting Public Values on Health*, 1995.

Simon Joss and John Durant define consensus conferences as 'a forum in which a group of lay people put questions about a scientific or technological subject of controversial political and social interest to experts, listen to the experts' answers, then reach a consensus about this subject and finally report their findings at a press conference'.[7]

In Denmark, subjects have included air pollution, childlessness, food irradiation and electronic identity cards, and the cost has been £35,000 to £50,000 per conference. The procedure is well-established in that country, and differs from citizens' juries in having a less representative method of selection, based on written applications. More time is spent in preparation, and the emphasis on consensus is an important difference. Consensus conferences are a variation on the theme of the informed citizen.

A Range of Innovation

These are not the only possible innovations. Other examples include:

* mediation groups which bring together groups which are in conflict over, for example, environmental issues, to see if through discussion differences can be reconciled or at least reduced

* new forms of public meetings designed to enable discussion in groups, rather than to structure meetings around platform and audience

* community forums in which authorities can reach out to diverse communities, remembering that as well as communities of place there are communities of interest

* stakeholder conferences in which all interested in an issue can be brought together in a variety of forms of discussion designed to identify areas for action

* teledemocracy which as time passes can have an increasing role in providing access for the public and involving the public

* involvement of citizens in scrutiny panels, village appraisal, environmental assessments.

---

7. JSimon Joss and John Durrant, *Consensus Conferences*, Science Museum Library, 1994.

All of these can enhance participatory democracy and strengthen representative democracy. There is also a case for direct democracy on specific issues. There is more of a tradition of referenda at local level than is often appreciated. There is a long history of referenda on libraries, local licensing options, Sunday opening of cinemas and private bills. Although most of these are in the past, the right of electors to call parish polls remains and what are, in effect, referenda have been instituted by the Conservative government for parents on options for grant maintained status and for tenants on the transfer of local authority housing stock. Some local authorities have recently held referenda on local issues such as the Sunday opening of leisure centres. The use of referenda on issues of community concern that lie outside the main framework of party political divides can be an exercise in citizenship, encouraging public discussion.

Towards Decentralisation

Strengthening democracy and public learning requires a learning government. The capacity of central government to constitute the basis for a learning system of government is limited. Many tiers in organisational hierarchies separate ministers from action and impact. Central government cannot easily encompass diversity of circumstance and achieve diversity in response. Yet learning comes from a recognition of diversity of need, diversity of aspiration and diversity of response. From uniformity one may learn little except of the scale of one's failure. One learns from diversity, of relative success and relative failure. A central government can achieve learning if it uses the diversity of local government as its base.

Participation is built more easily at local level than at national level and the evidence is that citizens are more ready to participate at that level. A commitment to the strengthening of participatory democracy is a commitment to decentralisation within the system of government, both to local authorities and within local authorities. Within local government, too, decentralisation and more effective local democracy involves a commitment to strengthen participatory democracy, through innovation in democratic practice for which a repertoire of approaches is being and can be developed.

In that repertoire citizens' juries are one example of a family of approaches constituting a public arena for discourse based on a representative sample of citizens. In that public arena, discourse can constitute the public domain for public learning and active citizenship.

Soundings

Soundings is a journal of politics and culture. It is a forum for ideas which aims to explore the problems of the present and the possibilities for a future politics and society. Its intent is to encourage innovation and dialogue in progressive thought. Half of each future issue will be devoted to debating a particular theme: topics in the pipeline include: The Media and Democracy, 'Young Britain' and an Election Special.

Why not subscribe?
Make sure of your copy

Subscription rates, 1997 (3 issues)

INDIVIDUAL SUBSCRIPTIONS
UK   £35.00
Rest of the World   £45.00

INSTITUTIONAL SUBSCRIPTIONS
UK   £70.00
Rest of the World   £80.00

Please send me one year's subscription starting with Issue Number _____

I enclose payment of £ _____

I wish to become a supporting subscriber and enclose a donation of £ _____

I enclose total payment of £ _____

Name _____

Address _____

_____

_____ Postcode _____

Please return this form with cheque or money order payable to Soundings and send to:

Soundings, c/o Lawrence & Wishart, 99A Wallis Road, London E9 5LN

Soundings

EDITORS
Stuart Hall
Doreen Massey
Michael Rustin

GUEST EDITOR
Maureen Mackintosh

CONTRIBUTORS
Elizabeth Bartlett
Brigid Benson
Roy Blackman
Carlo Borzaga
John Clarke
Maura Dooley
Will Hutton
Jane Falkingham
Paul Hirst
Ann Hudock
Paul Johnson
Michael Kenny
Charlie King
Sarabajaya Kumar
Richard Levins
Loretta Loach
Francie Lund
Maureen Mackintosh
Richard Minns
Anne Phillips
Anne Showstack Sassoon
Anne Simpson
Pam Smith
Tanya Stepan
John Stewart
Candy Stokes
Grahame Thompson
Gregory Warren Wilson
Liudmila Vasileva

The special theme of issue number four of **Soundings** is the public good. In particular, it looks at our apparent inability, in the late twentieth century, to imagine a public sphere which promotes the public good.

In examining the unravelling of old social settlements, the contributors, as well as analysing the huge problems of current policy, grapple with new opportunities for innovative practice, particularly in the voluntary – or 'third' – sector, and in new relationships between the private and public spheres.

Plus: globalisation, gender and equality, art in Bulgaria, poetry, more on Blair.

ISBN 0-85315-836-3

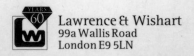
Lawrence & Wishart
99a Wallis Road
London E9 5LN

9 780853 158363 >